EDITION ONE

A BARRISTER'S GUIDE TO YOUR PERSONAL INJURY CLAIM

A LEGAL LIFELINE

—

JULIAN BENSON

—

A Barrister's Guide to Your Injury Claim – First Edition, 1.0, August 2012

Published by Julian Benson Publishing

Copyright © 2012 Julian Benson

ISBN: 978-0-9574064-0-7

The guide is intended to provide accurate information. It cannot and does not pretend to give advice in any specific situation. It is therefore not intended to be, and should not be taken as, a substitute for specific professional advice.

The moral right of Julian Benson to be identified as the author of this work has been asserted by him in accordance with the Copyright, Designs and Patents Act 1988.

All rights reserved. Except for the material freely available to download from the website www.abarristersguide.org.uk, no part of this publication may be reproduced, stored in a retrieval system, or transmitted in any form or by any means (electronic, mechanical, photocopying, recording or otherwise) without the prior written permission of the copyright holder.

FOREWORD

This is the first edition of "A Barrister's Guide to Your Personal Injury Claim".

My website www.abarristersguide.org.uk explains that the guide is intended to provide clear, authoritative and independent advice about all aspects of personal injury claims in England and Wales.

I have practiced in the field of personal injury law for over twenty years, working for injured individuals and for clients (often insurers) defending claims. Particularly when defending claims, I have encountered many examples of individuals being badly advised. For that reason, as well as providing advice, the guide will help you to ensure that you receive a professional service from your lawyers. That will, in turn, promote a fairer and quicker conclusion to your claim.

As and when changes take place which require amendments to this edition of the guide, these will be available to download free from the website. You must visit the website every few months to check for updates.

ACKNOWLEDGMENTS

I have had a great deal of help and support in writing this guide and setting up the website.

This includes an exceptional group of barrister colleagues and staff at Guildhall Chambers in Bristol, several of whom have assisted me to improve the guide. The same is true of several professional clients, friends and family, especially my wife Pennie. I am extremely grateful to all of them.

Jon and Nicola Payne of Noisy Little Monkey Ltd and Jamie Yearsley of Think Design have provided a superb professional and personal service in designing the website and advising me in many respects about the publication of the guide.

I bear the responsibility for any aspects of the guide which could be improved, and would invite any suggestions which I could incorporate when updating the guide, or in future editions.

CONTENTS

Part One:	Introduction And Overview	1
Section 1:	Aims of the guide	2
Section 2:	What you can expect from a claim	7
Section 3:	How does the law compensate me?	9

Part Two:	Your Relationship With Lawyers	13
Section 4:	The different lawyers you will encounter and their roles	14
Section 5:	Does it matter how you found your solicitor?	27
Section 6:	Do I have to keep the same legal representatives?	29
Section 7:	Finding new representatives	31
Section 8:	Funding a personal injury claim	33
Section 9:	Who will pay my compensation if I am successful, and why?	36
Section 10:	What aggravates insurers and how it can affect you	38
Section 11:	Why did the insurer video me?	42

Part Three:	What You Need To Know About The Law In Practice	45
Section 12:	Introduction to evidence	46
Section 13:	Pitfalls with expert evidence	52
Section 14:	What is 'causation' and why does it matter?	59

Part Four:	Putting The Claim Together	63
Section 15:	How you should approach the claim	64
Section 16:	Elements of the claim	66
Section 17:	The key litigation documents	72
Section 18:	Further stages in the litigation	77
Section 19:	Interim payments	83

Part Five:	**When And How Claims End**	**85**
Section 20:	When is it time to settle my claim?	86
Section 21:	Offers to settle	87
Section 22:	What if something goes wrong and/or I feel pressured to settle?	90
Section 23:	A conference after the evidence is complete	92
Section 24:	Joint settlement meetings	93
Section 25:	Mediation/Alternative dispute resolution	95
Section 26:	Trial	96
Section 27:	Appeal	98

Part Six:	**The Award And Effect Of Compensation**	**99**
Section 28:	Lump sum or periodical sum	100
Section 29:	Preserving your benefits after the claim has finished	102
Section 30:	Provisional compensation – a rare exception to finality in claims	103

Part Seven:	**Final Thoughts**	**105**
Section 31:	Final thoughts	106

Part Eight: Additional Materials	**107**
Explanation of terms in the guide	108
Stages in a typical injury claim	112
Questions for your solicitor - or replacement solicitor	113
Client checklists on liability and valuation issues	115

INTRODUCTION AND OVERVIEW

—
PART ONE
—

SECTION 1: AIMS OF THE GUIDE

THE CONTEXT OF INJURY LITIGATION

1. People get injured every day. Most injuries are simple accidents for which no one is at fault. However, some injuries are caused by fault, which gives rise to a possibility of compensation. The vast majority of such injuries arise from accidents on the road, in the workplace, or on land (or property) owned by another 'person' (whether an individual, a company, etc.).

2. It is rare for individuals to suffer more than one injury giving rise to a claim. Therefore, most injured individuals only become involved in a claim once, and the process seems a mystery.

3. Although lawyers are experienced in many aspects of the process which are (understandably) unfamiliar to non-lawyers, a central message of this guide is that the vast majority of the process is common sense.

4. Injured individuals often simply rely upon their lawyers to do the best for them because they have enough on their plate just to get through the day in their new circumstances.

5. It may very well be that most lawyers deserve that trust. This guide is intended to help you to ensure that is the case, and that you are getting high quality legal advice and support, and in a timely fashion. The process often seems to be taking place 'around' you, and to take an inexplicably long time to achieve progress. As I explain in **section 2**, there are often sensible reasons why progress is slow (for example, arranging medical examinations, or awaiting the outcome of treatment). However, you should be given a clear idea of the timescales involved, and reasons which prolong aspects of the claim. You should also be kept updated rather than feeling embarrassed to telephone for progress, then frustrated if there is no news to report: **section 4**.

AIMS OF THE GUIDE

6. Among the aims of the guide are:
   (a) To demystify the legal process, so that you understand the process and the legal framework, what to expect and what role to play;
   (b) To enable you to contribute to building a clear and reasonable claim,

which will maximise the prospect that you will receive reasonable compensation by a settlement;

(c) To assist you to assess the service that you are receiving from your own representatives, to identify problems early (so that they may be rectified), and ultimately, if the relationship breaks down, to replace your advisors.

GUIDANCE ABOUT THE PROCESS

7. The process of making a claim, described in **section 2**, can be stressful, not least because one person (you) is trying to recover a financial loss caused by another person (or organisation). The process inevitably involves, on your side, blame ('you caused my injury'), and demand ('you have cost me…'), and on the opposing side, rejection ('I did not hurt you' or 'you were partly at fault') and refusal ('I will not pay you that much…'). Those issues inevitably give rise to disputes, many of which can be resolved, usually leaving a few more difficult issues to try to resolve by settlement.

8. The guide is not intended to erect barriers between you and the party (usually an insurance company) most likely to pay your claim if it succeeds. Everyone wants to keep their insurance premiums down, and insurers are bound to try to root-out unreasonable claims and keep genuine claims to a reasonable level: **sections 9 - 11**.

9. If, however, there is animosity or suspicion between the parties, it will become significantly more stressful, and the claim will inevitably be more difficult to settle. The guide is intended to help you to understand, and avoid contributing to, such difficulties: **sections 15 - 17**.

WILL MY CASE 'GO TO COURT'

10. Many individuals ask "will my case go to Court?" They do not know what proportion of cases end with a 'trial' or why, and they are also understandably nervous about 'going to Court'. The simple fact is that a tiny proportion of claims end in a 'trial': **section 26**. However, it is almost always more sensible for your representatives to prepare your claim as if it was going to end in a trial – that way their work will be focussed on what the Claimant would have to prove to the Court. It is an excellent discipline, and it also helps to put together a claim which is persuasive to the Defendant, and therefore has a very good chance of achieving a good settlement.

11. In a nutshell, provided you are well advised, there is a very good chance that your claim will be settled at a reasonable level.

GUIDANCE IF YOUR REPRESENTATIVES LET YOU DOWN

12. This guide is not intended to drive a wedge between you and your representatives. Your interests and theirs ought to be the same: to achieve for you (almost always) by settlement, the highest sum in compensation which can reasonably be recovered. The fact that **section 6** discusses changing representatives, reflects the fact that in some cases, for a variety of reasons, the relationship breaks down, and if that does happen you need to know what to do next.

GUIDANCE AFTER YOUR CLAIM HAS BEEN CONCLUDED

13. This guide may be of assistance to some readers who have concluded their claims, and feel that they were badly advised/represented, or pressured to settle their claim against their wishes. I discuss these issues in **section 22**.

HOW TO USE THIS GUIDE

14. The guide is a tool. It will cover issues and ideas which may, at first glance, seem very complicated. Don't panic!

15. You are likely to get bogged down by some of the concepts, but after reading a section a couple of times, the ideas will become more familiar.

16. I suggest that you (and/or someone who you would like to be involved) try to read it, a section at a time. Remember that you do not have to memorise anything!

17. Do not expect to understand every paragraph straight away. I have dealt with some particularly important issues in great detail (for example as regards expert medical evidence – **section 13**). The best way to understand those issues is to try (at least to start with) to read the whole section at the same time.

18. There are issues that I have not been able to cover (or cover in detail) in the guide. For example whether you receive part of your damages in one

lump sum or in stages: **section 29**. These will require explanation from your advisors.

19. The guide should help you to understand the elements of your claim and the responsibilities of your representatives, to enable you to work together as an effective team, and present a well reasoned claim to the insurers, to maximise the chances of a swift, fair settlement with the minimum of stress.

20. In essence the guide should help you to approach a difficult process with information, confidence and optimism.

STRUCTURE OF THE GUIDE

21. The guide is written in 'parts', 'sections', 'subsections' and numbered paragraphs, to assist you to navigate the content, and to make it easier to identify and incorporate updating material, which will appear on the website.

EDITIONS AND UPDATES

22. The nature of the guide means that it will require updating, both to incorporate major changes in the system (such as the important changes which are likely to come into force in April 2013) as well as changes in the court rules and the law.

23. **All purchasers of the guide will be able to (and must) print off free updating materials from the website for the edition of the guide they have purchased.** From time to time, a new edition of the guide will be published, which will incorporate all of the changes since the previous edition.

ADDITIONAL MATERIALS AT THE END OF THE GUIDE

EXPLANATION OF TERMS IN THE GUIDE

24. A list of terms and a short explanation, so that you can remind yourself of them at a glance.

STAGES IN A TYPICAL INJURY CLAIM

25. A list of the stages in a typical injury claim, with references to the relevant sections in the guide.

QUESTIONS TO ASK YOUR INITIAL – OR REPLACEMENT - SOLICITOR

26. A list of questions for you to ask your first and/or replacement solicitor, so that you can maximise the prospect that he will represent you well. It may be rather unusual for a representative to be asked questions of this type by a client, but I cannot think why anyone should object to answering them.

27. Also, the answers will help you - at a very difficult time - to feel confident that you will be well represented.

CLIENT CHECKLISTS DEALING WITH LIABILITY AND VALUATION ISSUES

28. These checklists, taken in large part from **section 16**, are intended to help you to identify the sorts of evidence which your representatives will need when compiling your claim.

GENDER USED THROUGHOUT THE GUIDE

29. Lastly, and only because I am a man, I have used he/him throughout the guide.

SECTION 2: WHAT YOU CAN EXPECT FROM A CLAIM

THE AIM OF THE PROCESS

30. The aim of the law is stated very clearly: to return you as nearly as possible to the position you would have been in 'but for' the accident. Of course, that is virtually impossible in many cases. Your life may have been permanently changed by the injury you have suffered, whether because of a serious disability, or a less serious problem which nevertheless prevents you from undertaking (or enjoying) something which was important to your quality of life (whether that be running, swimming, long walks, or sex). It is very difficult to 'put a value' on such restrictions.

WHY IS THE PROCESS SO STRESSFUL?

31. Suffering an injury creates its own acute stress, often caused by immediate severe pain, dependence on others and uncertainty of the future.

32. Litigation often starts (in the sense that a person seeks representation) after the 'acute' phase of the injury, i.e. often after you return from hospital, or in less serious cases, when you return to work.

33. The injured person will then discover that the stress of the injury is aggravated, sometimes significantly, by the stress of litigation.

34. The legal process is 'adversarial' – that is to say that it is set up so that the parties are 'adversaries' (in opposition to one another). The claimant's task is to prove what injuries he suffered and what consequences those injuries have had (or may potentially have) on his work/career, his family and social life, and leisure pursuits. The 'person' defending the claim is very rarely the person who caused the injury (**section 9**). In almost every case, the person who you have to make a claim against is insured. Even though the person/organisation which caused the injury is named in the Court documents as "the defendant", the insurance company will very often conduct the defence.

35. The defendant's task is to challenge each aspect of the claim, so that it does not incur liability to pay claims which are not linked to the accident

(and/or are improperly claimed). It is therefore vital for you, and your representatives, to focus on the claims which are reasonably linked to the accident, described in greater detail in the section on causation (**section 14**).

BRACE YOURSELF – BE PREPARED TO DEAL WITH 'LOWS'

36. Letters from solicitors bearing bad or confusing news can arrive when you are at your lowest ebb. You are likely to have to undergo repeated examinations, going over the accident again and again, when the thing you most want is to put it behind you.

37. You may feel that experts who examine you are trying to trip you up, or confuse you, so that you feel as if you are the person 'on trial'.

38. There may be unexplained delays which make you feel 'out of the loop', even abandoned, and there may be long delays caused by the need to undergo treatment or appointments.

39. You may be told that there is surveillance film of you, which feels annoying, intrusive and unfair (**section 11**).

WHAT WILL THIS AWFUL PROCESS ACHIEVE FOR ME?

40. The legal process will, in most cases, provide:

    (a) An opportunity for you to have a clear, high quality medical diagnosis of your injury;

    (b) Treatment to maximise your recovery, (e.g. physiotherapy) funded with an interim payment (**section 19**);

    (c) A clear prognosis, informing you what, if any, long term effects the accident may have upon you;

    (d) A fair and reasonable level of compensation for the losses caused by the accident.

41. As you will quickly learn, involvement with the law will not make you better! But the process is worthwhile. It will enable you to achieve reasonable financial protection against the consequences of your injury. But from the start, you will need to be as calm, patient and resolute as possible.

SECTION 3: HOW DOES THE LAW COMPENSATE ME?

MONEY SPENT AND MONEY LOST

42. The law is generally good at replacing money you have lost as a result of your injuries (typically earnings), and money you have legitimately spent (typically on treatment, aids/equipment, assistance, travel, painkillers, etc): see generally **section 16**.

43. In most personal injury cases, by far and away the largest part of the claim is past and future earnings loss. However, in certain other very serious cases, the following can be a substantial part of the claim:

    (a) Future physical care and assistance – for example in claims where there are serious ongoing restrictions caused by the accident injuries;

    (b) Future 'case management' (essentially 'care co-ordination') and care in a serious brain injury case, where the injured person may require substantial daytime and night time support;

    (c) Prosthetics (artificial limbs) in an amputation claim, where the injured person is keen to maximise independence and activities.

PAIN AND SUFFERING AND LOSS OF AMENITY

44. The compensation awarded for the actual injury (or injuries), and its consequences is called the award for 'pain, suffering and loss of amenity' ('amenity' meaning loss of enjoyment of life), also described as PSLA, or 'general damages' (all meaning exactly the same thing).

45. Estimating PSLA used to be a case of looking at hundreds of old decisions and estimating where your claim fitted in to the picture. Since the early 1990's judges and practitioners have been assisted in estimating awards by the 'Judicial Studies Board ('JSB') Guidelines' (a booklet, revised over 20 years), which provides brackets of awards for physical and psychological injuries.

46. In my experience, most people think that the compensation for their injury is far too low. Unfortunately, the general level of awards in the JSB Guidelines is extremely difficult to challenge.

REDUCTIONS TO COMPENSATION - (I) CONTRIBUTORY FAULT

47. In many cases, in which the cause of an accident is obvious, liability is settled between the parties very early on. In other situations, the defendant may accept that they are primarily 'liable' (i.e. at fault) for the accident, but they consider that the claimant contributed to his injuries and financial losses. This is a very frequent situation in workplace claims and road traffic accident ('RTA') claims (perhaps because the claimant was driving too fast - or at work was taking a risk known to be dangerous).

48. In such situations, you and your advisers will have to consider how 'liability'/fault should be 'split' between the parties. At trials, the Court usually divides liability in proportions such as 50:50; 67:33: 75:25 in favour of one or other party.

49. If contributory negligence (or fault) is alleged against you, it is obviously important for you:

    (a) to understand the reasons why you are being asked to consider sharing the blame, and

    (b) to be given persuasive reasons for agreeing what proportion of 'fault' your representatives consider you ought to accept. See also, **section 22 and 23**.

REDUCTIONS TO COMPENSATION - (II) MITIGATION OF LOSS

50. In every claim the injured person has a duty to act reasonably to reduce the impact of the accident. That duty is referred to as the 'duty to mitigate'. The duty arises in a number of ways and it is really best thought of as a part of the idea of 'causation', which is explained in **section 14**. Essentially, if a person acts reasonably he is very unlikely to have failed to mitigate his loss, and his damages are therefore unlikely to be reduced.

51. The concept of mitigation means different things in relation to different aspects of the claim. One aspect of mitigation would be to replace a damaged item at a reasonable cost. That seems obvious. Another example would concern a person's decision to take a job which paid less, was less pleasant (or convenient) and less skilled than his pre-accident work, in order to achieve some earnings. If the person decided not to accept such a job,

then if the claim did not settle the Court would have to decide whether that was 'reasonable'.

52. When assessing 'reasonableness' in the context of 'mitigation of loss' the Court does not set the standard very high. It appreciates that people may make imperfect decisions - in the above example, 'hanging on' for a better job might have been reasonable. That will depend upon the precise circumstances, and will require detailed evidence and skilled advice.

53. Also, in the specific context of medical treatment, the law is very reluctant indeed to criticise a person for failing to undergo invasive treatment (such as an operation requiring a general anaesthetic).

54. It might be possible for an insurer to argue that someone whose symptoms were likely to be cured, or very substantially improved, with a short course of physiotherapy, had failed to mitigate their loss by not having the course. That might in turn enable the insurer to prevent the person from recovering their earnings loss after the physiotherapy would have finished.

55. On the other hand, it is very unlikely indeed that deciding not to undertake an operation would be considered a failure to mitigate.

YOUR RELATIONSHIP WITH LAWYERS

—
PART TWO
—

SECTION 4: THE DIFFERENT LAWYERS YOU WILL ENCOUNTER AND THEIR ROLES

HOW DO 'LAWYERS', 'SOLICITORS', AND 'BARRISTERS' RELATE TO MY CASE?

56. This is a question which individuals often want to ask but feel too embarrassed: are there two or more different types of lawyer, and if so – why, and what do they do?

THE SOLICITOR

57. In a nutshell, a personal injury solicitor works in a 'firm' or 'partnership'. Solicitors are lawyers, who have met the qualifications and training requirements of the Law Society (**see the links on the website**).

WHAT DOES THE SOLICITOR DO?

58. In general terms, the solicitor builds and shapes your claim. They start by meeting you (and/or getting you to complete a detailed questionnaire), explaining their terms of business, learning about the accident, and gathering factual and expert evidence to support the claim.

HOW DOES A SOLICITOR ATTRACT/OBTAIN WORK?

59. A firm of solicitors traditionally attracted work by 'word of mouth' recommendations and by local presence (e.g. on the High Street). More recently, some (especially large) firms of solicitors offering personal injury services have obtained work via referral agreements with other businesses. An example might be an agreement to pay an insurance broker (or claims company) a fee to refer an injured person to them (a 'referral fee'), a trade union who refers its injured members to a firm that has been successful in tendering for that work, or a company who advertises for injured individuals to contact it (or 'signs up' people in shopping centres, etc).

60. The latter are 'claims companies', which often advertise heavily on television/radio, the internet, and newspapers, and refer individuals who contact them, for a fee, to firms of solicitors with whom they have a commercial agreement. The Government intends to abolish these "referral fees" (and make other radical changes to the funding of injury claims) from April 2013

onwards – the website will be updated to ensure that you are kept informed.

61. There are other, often smaller, more traditional firms of solicitors, where a small number of individuals conduct personal injury litigation. Those individuals probably receive their work from the traditional recommendations, local presence, or indeed because they are highly specialised in a particular field (perhaps occupational diseases, or pain syndromes). It may not have been possible (or desirable) for them to pay fees for referrals, but there is no reason why a solicitor in a smaller firm should be less likely to represent you with excellence.

62. Clearly, in a large firm, there may be a 'pool' of knowledge solicitors can usefully share, but equally, an expert in a small firm may be able to devote more time to your claim than might be possible in a large firm, where each solicitor may have a very large caseload or might have to spend a significant amount of time supervising junior staff instead of on his own cases.

63. It is worth keeping in mind that most of the firms which represent injured individuals advertise themselves as 'specialists in personal injury litigation'.

64. Given that you have already suffered an injury, you need to feel relaxed about the way your claim is being handled. So, without being overly critical, try to judge whether you feel as if you are a valued client:

    (a) Who is dealing with your claim - a trained lawyer with experience? (see later on in this section);
    (b) Does he respond reasonably quickly to your calls, emails or letters?
    (c) Does he deal sensibly with your concerns?
    (d) Is your case progressing, and if not, have you been given reasons for any delays?
    (e) Have you received an interim payment, and if not, what is the reason? (**see section 19**);
    (f) Have you been sent to be examined by a medical expert who is a specialist in the injury you have suffered? (**see section 13**).

65. If answering those questions does give rise to concerns, you should tell your solicitor, so that they can be addressed. If that does not happen, you should consider moving on (**see section 6**).

THE PEOPLE YOU MAY ENCOUNTER IN THE SOLICITOR'S OFFICE

66. Firms of solicitors also employ people who have different qualifications but can still provide useful services (at a lesser wage cost to the firm). The typical composition of a solicitors firm may include all of the following individuals acting for an injured person:

(a)	Equity Partner	a solicitor who owns part ('the equity' or value) of the firm, usually with others, and receives a share of the firm's annual profits;
(b)	Salaried Partner	a solicitor (or more rarely legal executive) who is granted the prestigious title 'partner', but does not co-own the firm, and is therefore paid a salary;
(c)	Associate Solicitor	an experienced solicitor who is usually looking to become a partner;
(d)	Consultant	usually an experienced solicitor, or legal executive;
(e)	Solicitor	a lawyer qualified in accordance with the standards and requirements of the Law Society (**see the link on the website**);
(f)	Assistant Solicitor	a fully qualified but less experienced solicitor;
(g)	Trainee Solicitor	an apprentice solicitor;
(h)	Legal Executive	a lawyer qualified in accordance with the standards and requirements of the Chartered Institute of Legal Executives (**see the link on the website**), who is able to undertake all work that may be undertaken by a solicitor under the supervision of the solicitor;
(i)	Litigation executive	a person who does not have legal qualifications, but may be experienced and knowledgeable;
(j)	Paralegal	often similar to a litigation executive;

DO THE SAME SOLICITORS ACT FOR INJURED INDIVIDUALS AND INSURERS?

67. In recent years an increasing number of firms of solicitors have tended to represent either injured individuals or defendants (i.e. insurers), but not both. This has lead to an increase in the sense of 'us' and 'them' on both sides.

68. The same trend has unfortunately developed in relation to expert witnesses, who tend increasingly to provide evidence to one 'side' or the other, despite the fact that the expert's duty is, above all, to the Court (**see section 13**).

THE 'BARRISTER' – ALSO REFERRED TO AS 'COUNSEL'

69. A barrister, just like a solicitor, is a lawyer. They have a long and interesting history (**see the link to 'Middle Temple' on the website**). There is still something of a mystique about barristers, probably because they still wear a very historical costume in court, the best known parts of which are a horsehair wig and a long black gown.

DIFFERENT TERMS FOR DIFFERENT BARRISTERS

70. There are only two 'levels' of barrister. About 90% are 'just' barristers, who are also known within the profession as 'junior counsel'. About 10% of barristers are 'senior counsel', who are also known as 'Queen's Counsel' (or 'QC'). Being appointed QC is recognition of excellence and seniority within the profession. As a rough guide, in personal injury work, QCs are appointed after about 25 years in practice.

71. There are a number of different names for QCs, including, 'silks' (because they wear a silk gown), and 'leading counsel'. The phrase 'leading counsel' reflects the fact that sometimes a silk and a junior may be instructed together (the silk is said to 'lead' the junior). These are typically in cases involving many complex legal issues, a large volume of documentation, or a very high value claim, such as the multi-million pound lifelong care claims seen in catastrophic brain injury cases.

72. There are many very skilled and experienced barristers who, for a number of reasons, choose not to 'apply for silk' (one reason is because so few cases end in a trial, that it is very difficult to gather the number of judge's

references required for the application; another is because there is not enough local work at the QC level).

73. Within the profession, more experienced juniors are sometimes known as 'senior juniors'. It follows from what I have explained, that in the vast majority of personal injury cases, you will be represented by a barrister who is not a QC.

QUALIFYING TO BECOME A BARRISTER

74. A barrister must meet the qualifications and training requirements of the Bar Standards Board (**see the link on the website**).

75. Traditionally, barristers have been considered the 'advocates' among lawyers, i.e. the lawyers who actually present a case in Court. In injury claims, there are often several 'hearings' during the progress of a case, which justify the use of a barrister, because of the importance of the issues for the outcome of the claim.

76. Barristers are also routinely asked by solicitors to consider the nature of evidence required to establish elements of the claim, and to meet the client 'in conference' to discuss the strengths and weaknesses of such evidence and how any gaps might be filled.

77. Most barristers are self employed. They work in offices called 'a barrister's chambers', or 'set or chambers', and they pool their administrative expenses. The vast majority of barristers receive their work from solicitors, in the form of 'instructions to counsel' (discussed below).

THE 'CAB RANK' RULE

78. Barristers generally operate under what is still known as the 'cab-rank rule'. In other words, where the following conditions are met, he must – like the taxi waiting for a passenger on the taxi rank – accept the 'job', however attractive or unattractive it is, providing:
    (a) The work falls within his area of expertise, and he is available;
    (b) The work is appropriate to his experience and seniority;
    (c) His fees will be paid whatever the outcome of the case.

79. The rule does not apply in a case in which the barrister will only be paid if his client wins – i.e. in a conditional fee agreement ('CFA') case – also known as "no win-no fee", where the legal fees are only payable – i.e. are conditional upon – winning. Most personal injury claims are funded by legal expenses insurance or conditional fee agreement ('CFA') (**see section 8**).

HOW DO BARRISTERS RECEIVE THEIR WORK?

80. The technical terminology is that solicitors 'instruct' barristers, which really means 'invite them to undertake work'. In practical terms, this means that the solicitor sends a file of papers to the barrister, with a document ('instructions to counsel') which explains the case, and what work the solicitor is requesting the barrister to perform.

WHEN SHOULD A BARRISTER BE INSTRUCTED?

81. Some solicitors prefer to gather all of the evidence before instructing a barrister, and some prefer to involve the barrister earlier on. Barristers almost always prefer to be involved earlier, rather than later, so that they can have some input into evidential issues before it becomes difficult to do so (e.g. when memories are less sharp, a witness might no longer be located, or when there is little time for the barrister to help to 'shape the case' before a settlement meeting or trial: (**see section 24 - 26**).

82. It is sometimes difficult to know when exactly to instruct a barrister. The solicitor may consider that they will not recover the costs of using a barrister early on, because it might later be thought unreasonable to have involved a barrister at that stage. This will generally depend upon the amount of compensation at stake, the complexity of issues concerning 'fault' and 'quantum', and the specific issue counsel is asked to consider. As a rule of thumb, in claims with a value of over £50,000, there is unlikely to be criticism of a solicitor who involves a barrister at an early stage.

CAN BOTH BARRISTERS IN A CASE BE IN THE SAME CHAMBERS?

83. One odd feature of the barrister's position is that he may be instructed in a case in which a member of his chambers acts for the opposing party. This happens more often in the regions, where there are fewer specialist barristers than in London. From the outside, it can appear unsettling that your barrister

is a professional colleague (even a good friend) of the opposing barrister. In practice, providing the barrister acts in accordance with their professional duties, to represent your interests fearlessly, then those issues ought not to matter.

84. It is always sensible for the barrister to tell his client if he is a colleague of the opposing barrister, and for that matter, whether he has worked with the opposing defendant solicitor or insurer.

POTENTIAL TENSION BETWEEN SOLICITORS AND BARRISTERS

85. As the barrister depends upon a solicitor to send him work, even if his only duty is to represent his client fearlessly (within the rules of Court) he is likely to want to be instructed again by that solicitor. This could cause a tension for the barrister if he considers that the solicitor has made an important mistake in the case. If he points out the mistake to the client, that could affect his relationship with the solicitor. If he does not, he is not representing his client's interests.

86. This tension might be even greater if a barrister depended upon a small number of solicitors for a great deal of his work, or where the solicitor and barrister (or even the barrister's chambers) have reached an arrangement for the barrister/s to provide fixed fee advisory work in return for a guarantee volume of cases. It is well worth checking with your solicitors whether such an arrangement exists, and whether they will permit you to obtain a second opinion from a specialist barrister who is not part of such an arrangement.

RESOLVING THE TENSION

87. The duties of the barrister (and solicitor) are very clearly to represent the client's interests. If either has made a significant mistake, there is no doubt that you should be informed immediately.

TRUST: THE CORNERSTONE OF YOUR RELATIONSHIP WITH YOUR LAWYERS

88. You must be able to trust your barrister and your solicitor. They must earn your trust by demonstrating the professionalism of the service they are providing.

89. One way to establish trust is to meet your barrister and solicitor together quite early in the process in 'a conference' (or 'con' (!) for short), to discuss all of the areas of the claim. (Even if that is difficult to arrange, you should be able to have a multi-party telephone conference to cover the same ground).

90. It is the barrister's job, like any other professional person, to give you clear, reasoned advice, uncluttered by jargon. If you do not understand anything you have been told, that is almost certainly a failing of the barrister, not you, and you must ask for clearer explanations and reasoning.

91. If for any reason (including his inability to justify an opinion) you feel that the barrister selected for you will not represent you as you would wish, you should request that your solicitor selects another barrister, or even that the solicitor suggests a couple of alternatives, and you can look at their profiles on their websites. The sorts of reasons that may cause you concern include if you do not feel the barrister has read his 'instructions' carefully (i.e. does not 'know' your case) or if he has not listened to you in discussions (i.e. does not 'understand' your case).

92. Once again, it is also worth ensuring that you are not restricted for any reason, by the choice of barrister, particularly if you are seeking a second opinion. Also, you may prefer to ask for a second opinion from a barrister who is recommended in one of the independent guides (mentioned below). If that is refused to you, it may be time to reconsider your position with your own solicitor.

WHERE TO FIND INDEPENDENT RECOMMENDATIONS
ABOUT LAWYERS

93. Most lawyers, whether firms of solicitors or barristers' chambers, have websites. These may have CV's of individuals and quotations from clients (testimonials of service), which can be helpful in explaining why they are well placed to assist the injured person. However, do be aware that such websites are not independent. They are essentially an 'advertisement' for that lawyer. Just like any other advert, it is important to assess what you read, rather than just to accept everything in the advert.

94. An odd feature of a barrister's position is that even though he is competing against other barristers for work, he is restricted in how he may advertise for work. For example, barristers are not permitted to advertise 'rates of success' as a way to attract further work.

95. There are also independently published 'professional directories' (such as 'Chambers & Partners' and 'The Legal 500' – **see links to both on the website**) which make comments and recommendations about solicitors and barristers which can be helpful. Being listed in a directory is a useful indicator of quality, but it is no guarantee. Similarly, not being listed does not mean that your representatives will fail to provide a professional service. Of course, many organisations offering legal services will have websites, which will include testimonials, which may be useful. But at the end of the day, and with the help of the 'guide', you must maintain your awareness of your claim as it progresses to ensure that you are continuing to receive the excellent service you deserve – and which fees paid to your lawyers reflect.

TWO MORE REASONS WHY TRUST IS SO IMPORTANT

96. As I have said at the start of the guide, most lawyers do their best for clients and provide a professional service.

97. The aim of the guide is to explain the process comprehensively, and for that reason I will briefly comment on two further points which re-emphasize the need to establish a relationship of trust with your solicitor.

98. First, as it is rare for a person to suffer more than one accident giving rise to a claim, it is very unlikely that he will ever need to use the solicitor (or barrister) again. Likewise, the lawyers are unlikely to encounter the client again. Therefore, unless the solicitor is a local firm, or acts for the person more generally, there is less obvious incentive for the lawyers to achieve the best result they can.

99. Second, in England and Wales, the injured person generally receives all of their damages. Their representatives are not (yet) permitted to 'take' any part of the injured person's damages (compared to the USA, where the fees of the lawyers are often permitted to be a portion of the damages – known as a 'contingency fee').

100. It follows that there is no financial incentive for your representatives to achieve the highest reasonable award for you. It is to be hoped that they are motivated by their professional duties and pride. However, it is possible that for whatever reason (overworked, underpaid, under-qualified or unmotivated) your representatives will not do their best for you.

101. Those are all reason why it is so important that your representatives earn and deserve your trust.

THE LEGAL BASIS OF THE RELATIONSHIP WITH A SOLICITOR AND BARRISTER

102. Shortly after your initial contact (whether that is by telephone, email, letter or a face to face meeting), the solicitor will send you a letter setting out the proposed terms of the relationship between you. This should explain the relationship in some detail, including the solicitor's fees. This document should help you to understand such issues as:

    (a) Will the solicitor's firm pay for medical reports and other 'disbursements' incurred during the claim?

    (b) Will there be any deductions by the solicitor's firm from any interim payments that the defendant agrees, or that are ordered by the Court? **(see section 19)**

    (c) At the end of the claim, will you receive all of the damages agreed with the defendant (or ordered by the Court) or might you have any liability to pay 'costs' (i.e. the legal and other fees of you own advisors, or those of the other side) out of the sum you are awarded?

    (d) How soon will you receive your final award of damages after the claim ends?

103. Remember that your solicitor and barrister have a duty to provide you with the level of service to be expected from someone holding themselves out as having expertise in personal injury cases.

COURTS AND JUDGES

104. Personal injury claims which are not settled before the three year period generally permitted within which the court case must be started, are then managed (and in rare cases decided at trial) by judges.

105. Personal injury claims are 'civil cases' (as opposed, for example, to criminal cases). As such, they are dealt with by the 'civil courts' (rather than, for example the Crown Court, which deals with criminal cases).

106. There are two 'levels' of civil court where your claim may be handled: the County Court and the High Court.

THE COUNTY COURTS

107. The County Courts are based in regional cities and towns, and deal with the vast majority of personal injury cases, from small claims to high value claims. The location of your nearest County Court can be found using the Courts Service website (**see the link on the website**).

THE HIGH COURT AND DISTRICT REGISTRIES OF THE HIGH COURT

108. The High Court deals with the most complex and/or highest value cases. It is based at the 'Royal Courts of Justice' in the Strand, in London. You will probably have seen the building on television or in the press many times.

109. Although it is of more historical interest, and is not something which will affect you at all, personal injury claims are dealt with in one part (or 'Division') of the High Court, known historically as the 'Queens Bench Division' (or 'QBD').

110. As well as its base in London, the High Court has bases (best thought of as 'branches') outside London. These are called 'District Registries of the High Court'.

111. The High Court District Registries are confusingly located in the same buildings as the County Court. Also, as very few District Registries have 'their own' High Court judges, the same judges (who are granted special permission to do so) deal often deal with High Court and County Court cases in District Registries.

WHO ARE THE JUDGES?

112. Judges are (almost always) former solicitors and barristers. The vast majority of District Judges are former solicitors, and the vast majority of County

Court and High Court Judges are former barristers. There are also some part-time judges who 'sit' as judges for a few weeks a year, and otherwise work as solicitors and barristers.

113. Judges of differing seniority have separate titles and are addressed accordingly in court:

Court	Judge	Title	Called
High	High Court Judge	Mr Justice Smith	My Lord
High (London)	Master	Master Smith	Master
High (London)	Deputy Master	Deputy Master Smith	Master
High District Registry	District Judge	District Judge Smith	Sir
County	Circuit* Judge	His Honour Judge Smith	Your Honour
County	Recorder**	Mr Recorder Smith	Your Honour
County	District Judge	District Judge Smith	Sir
County	Deputy District Judge^	Deputy District Judge Smith	Sir

(*For historical reasons, relating to the geographical region, or 'circuit' over which they preside, senior County Court Judges are also known as a Circuit Judges)
(** A Recorder is a practicing lawyer who sits as a Circuit Judge a few weeks a year)
(^ A Deputy District Judge is a practicing lawyer who sits as a District Judge a few weeks a year)

114. In general terms, after the claim is started, it is managed by the Court at short hearings, often by telephone. These hearings are almost always dealt with by District Judges in the County Court (and District Registries) and by Masters in the High Court in London. (**see also section 17/18, and 'stages in a typical injury claim', after the end of the guide**).

115. If the case ends in a trial, it will (apart from a tiny minority of specific claims) be 'heard' (i.e. decided) by a judge at a trial (see **section 26**). In smaller claims (including 'small claims' and fast track claims': **section 18**) the judge at trial is likely to be a District Judge. In larger claims in the County Court (i.e. multi-track claims: **section 18**) the judge is likely to be a Circuit Judge. In the High Court in London the judge is likely to be a High Court Judge. In the High Court District Registries, the judge is likely to be a Circuit Judge sitting as (i.e. having permission to perform the role of) a High Court Judge.

116. All barristers have to remember to address the judge in the capacity in which the judge is 'sitting', so that a Circuit Judge sitting as a High Court Judge is addressed as 'My Lord, and not 'Your Honour'!

SECTION 5: DOES IT MATTER HOW YOU FOUND YOUR SOLICITOR?

REFERRAL, ADVERTISING OR RECOMMENDATION

117. Providing your solicitor does his job properly it does not matter. But it is worth keeping in mind how the relationship started. If you were referred to your solicitor by an insurance company, it may be because the solicitor and insurer had a 'business deal' between them (i.e. the solicitor has paid for you to be referred to them). That may mean the solicitor has expertise in personal injury litigation. It may not. The same is true of a firm you choose through an advertisement. What matters is that:
    (a) You are aware that a lawyer calling himself a personal injury specialist does not necessarily make him one;
    (b) Even if he is a personal injury specialist, he must earn your trust by:
        (i) communicating with you regularly;
        (ii) answering your questions – with reasons you understand – not 'fobbing you off';
        (iii) never putting your interests second: you do not want to know that they have been too busy to do something that should have been done for you;
        (iv) recognising that it is their privilege to have you as a client is the crux of the relationship – after all your case is enabling your representatives to earn their living.

DOES IT MATTER IF MY SOLICITOR IS NOT LOCAL?

118. This largely depends on the service provided to you. If you feel 'out on a limb' then you are probably not receiving the service you want or need.

119. As explained in **section 13**, it is imperative that the medical expert/s provide high quality specialist evidence. Local solicitors often know excellent local experts. Solicitors who are based many miles away from where you live often rely upon agencies to provide medical experts for litigation. Some of those experts may be excellent, but it is very difficult to know in advance, unless for example, the solicitor knows the expert through experience, because they specialise in a particular field, or as the result of a reliable recommendation from another lawyer or expert.

120. However, it is also possible that a solicitor has to take 'pot luck' with the agency's recommendation, or a local named expert. It is perhaps obvious, but worth stating, that it is crucial that no part of your claim is based upon pot luck.

121. In any case where your solicitor is using a medical expert for the first time, then they ought to ask him for a recent report (with the client's name deleted), so that your solicitor can be reassured that the expert's reports are high quality.

CONTINUITY AND OTHER ISSUES OF SERVICE

122. It is vital that you have as much continuity as possible from your representatives. It is very often the case that in a substantial or long-running case, 'your' solicitor could change (maternity leave, redundancy, promotion, change of firms, even retirement).

123. It is very difficult to maintain a good working relationship with 'your' firm if the fee earner changes routinely during the course of your claim. This is not uncommon. If you are told that someone else is 'taking over' your case, ask for a meeting with the new solicitor straight away to review the case. That meeting is your opportunity for you to evaluate whether the new solicitor has got to grips with the case and will protect your interests.

WHAT SHOULD I DO IF I FEEL LET DOWN?

124. If you feel let down for any reason and you do not address the situation, your trust in your representatives will start to erode. That feeling is difficult to reverse, and because trust is so important, my advice is never ignore a failure which matters to you. Tell your representatives and (politely) demand a professional service.

125. Given that the world of litigation is itself unfamiliar, the last thing most litigants want is to have the stress of second-guessing whether they are receiving a good service (or even feeling that they should change representatives). However, in some cases, there comes a time when you must bite the bullet.

SECTION 6: DO I HAVE TO KEEP THE SAME LEGAL REPRESENTATIVES?

WHEN MIGHT I BECOME CONCERNED ABOUT THE HANDLING OF MY CLAIM?

126. In **section 5** I discussed potential concerns you might have about the overall conduct of your claim. In addition, you may be concerned if your representatives suggest that your claim is unusual, complicated, or must be settled for compensation which seems totally inadequate to you.

127. A simple example might be an orthopaedic injury (e.g. fracture or soft tissue) which is expected to, but does not, recover within, say, a year. The orthopaedic expert may not be able to explain the basis of your ongoing symptoms from the perspective of his medical knowledge.

128. In that situation, one solicitor might consider that the claim should be settled on the basis of one year of losses – especially if the defendant has made a reasonable offer to settle on that basis. Another solicitor, more committed and professional, is likely to consider obtaining further medical evidence, before accepting what could be a woefully inadequate offer if the continuing symptoms are linked to the accident.

129. If your solicitor instead seems to want to settle at all costs without clarifying the medical position, you may very well want to consider contacting another solicitor.

IS IT VERY DIFFICULT TO CHANGE SOLICITORS?

130. It is bound to be stressful to have to change your solicitor, but if you can find a firm who will look after your interests properly, it is bound to be better in the long run.

131. It is less difficult to change representatives than you might think, although it is much easier to do so earlier in the claim – so that the new lawyers can make their mark on the way the claim is resolved (particularly obtaining additional medical evidence).

132. You can instruct alternative representatives later on but that can present more difficulties. A new solicitor will understandably be reluctant to step in when there is little prospect of recovering their reasonable fees from your opponent, which is more likely to be the case the later you make the change.

133. If you do want to make a change, there can also be funding issues to resolve: **section 8**. You can explore this, and all of the other issues, with the new solicitor before deciding how to continue.

SECTION 7: FINDING NEW REPRESENTATIVES

FINDING A NEW SOLICITOR

134. Your existing solicitor will probably not want to lose you as a client, unless your case, or you (!), are regarded as very difficult. He will almost certainly not recommend a different firm to you, and your barrister may also find it very difficult to do so, having received your case from that solicitor, and given that his contact with you is via the solicitor.

135. It may well be that you were 'referred' to the solicitor by your own legal expense insurer (e.g. via your motor/household insurance). If you do not have a sensible reason for wanting to change, then the insurer may be unhappy to allow another firm (it does not know) to represent you. By the same token, you will not want to jeopardise your 'legal expenses cover'.

136. These problems seem difficult, but there are almost always straightforward ways to change solicitor without losing your legal expense cover. The best advice is not to change your representatives unless you have a good reason.

137. When seeking a replacement firm, perhaps the first thing to do is to ask family and friends who may know someone who has had a better experience than you with a claim. If that does not help, then if you have access to the internet, you might search for solicitors, using your locality, or your injury, to focus the search. Look for websites which have testimonials or blogs, so that you can really feel that the person you approach knows what they are doing!

138. Then before you make the change, ask the second solicitor to answer the questions at the end of the guide, in writing, to reassure you that you should make the change.

FINDING A NEW BARRISTER

139. This should be easier, especially if you have changed solicitor, as the new firm will probably have a relationship with several barristers, and even several barristers' chambers. Once again, remember that you want a barrister to satisfy you that he has thoroughly read and understood your claim, and that he will represent your interests fearlessly, with the skill of someone claiming specialist ability as an advocate.

140. It is also worth noting that if you are happy with your barrister you should tell your new solicitor and ask that the same barrister continues to be instructed.

SECTION 8: FUNDING A PERSONAL INJURY CLAIM

INTRODUCTION TO FUNDING ISSUES

141. **The following section deals with funding issues which apply in July 2012. However, a range of radical changes is very likely to be introduced in April 2013. You will need to visit the website and download updated material to ensure that your knowledge is up to date.**

142. Every litigant has to have some means of funding their claim. Put another way, all lawyers and medics want to be paid, and they are expensive! To put that into context, the Court publishes rates of payment for solicitors (and others working in solicitor's firms) in different geographical areas, and at different levels of seniority (known as 'grades'). At the commencement of your relationship with the solicitor, he will inform you in writing of the rates of payment they charge.

143. In very broad terms there are presently two main methods of funding a claim. First, there is 'Before the Event' insurance ('BTE'), the 'event' being your accident. This is a fund of money available to you to pay the costs of your own lawyers, and the defendant's lawyers (if you lose the case). It is also known as 'legal expense insurance' ('LEI').

144. Second, there is a 'no win–no fee' agreement, also known as a Conditional Fee Agreement ('CFA'), the 'condition' being 'success' of your claim. The CFA is coupled with insurance (called 'After the Event' ('ATE') insurance) which is intended to pay the defendant's costs if your claim is not successful.

145. Both types of cover will have their own specific terms (within a 'policy' document), and both will have financial limits.

BTE INSURANCE IN MORE DETAIL

146. BTE cover is legal cover often provided by your household or motor insurance. Typically, BTE cover will have a limit of £50,000, which is likely to be adequate for a moderate sized claims. You will have paid the 'premium' for your BTE cover as a part of the premium for your motor/home policy.

147. As far as the fault/liability side of the claim is concerned, the insurer will usually continue to indemnify (i.e. 'cover') your legal and expert costs, and the defendant's costs, as long as a barrister (or sometimes a solicitor) certifies the chances of winning are reasonable (sometimes this might be "over 51%", or "over 60%", depending on the policy, and the figure may differ for the 'liability' and 'valuation' parts of the claim).

148. As far as the valuation of your claim is concerned (or 'quantum' as lawyers call it), the BTE insurer usually continues to fund the claim until the defendant makes an offer which you are unlikely to 'beat' at a trial. Once again, it is usually your solicitor or barrister who advises the insurer of the chances of beating any offer, as the claim proceeds. This is very important, and is dealt with in **section 22**.

ATE INSURANCE

149. ATE is an insurance policy purchased after the accident to provide 'cover' for your opponent's costs and (often) your own side's out of pocket expenses, called 'disbursements', such as the cost of expert's reports, paying for Court Fees, and gathering medical records. Providing you 'win' your claim (i.e. you settle for a higher sum than the defendant's best previous offer, or at trial beat the best offer) the ATE insurance will not be called upon.

150. Most solicitors will help you find a suitable policy. The premiums differ depending on the merits of the claim (a rear-end traffic accident is likely to cost a lot less than a complicated workplace claim) and the stage your case has reached when you take out the policy.

151. ATE providers generally 'defer' the payment of the premium until the claim has finished, but in actual fact do not ever recover the premium from you if your claim is unsuccessful. In almost all 'winning cases', you will be able to recover the insurance premium from the defendant, when the costs of the case are being decided or settled at the end of the case, providing it was at a reasonable market level. The radical changes proposed by the Government, which are likely to come into force in April 2013, will have a very marked effect upon every aspect of funding for injury claims. You must download free updates dealing with these issues from the website.

152. Once again, the lawyers have a duty to keep the insurer informed of the merits of your claim as the evidence develops, and of any offers to settle which are received.

BTE AND ATE TOGETHER

153. There are situations in which both types of insurance are combined. This is often in a substantial claim, where the costs are clearly going to exceed the limit of the BTE cover. In that case, your solicitor will find additional, or 'top-up' ATE cover.

FINAL WORD ON FUNDING

154. Before BTE, and CFA's with ATE, litigants often had to fund a claim themselves, with their savings, a re-mortgage of their home, and the like. That would create a pressure all of its own when an offer was received which might expose the litigant to pay months or years of the defendant's costs personally. But in that situation, the client's decision would have been the final decision.

155. In the world of BTE insurance, and CFA's with ATE insurance, the insurer can decide to withdraw their financial 'cover' if your lawyers do not persuade them that it is reasonable for the claim to continue. Ultimately they cannot stop you from continuing the claim, but if you do so, then from that time onwards you will be exposed to the future costs which to that point were covered by the insurance. That is another critical reason why you must know and trust your representatives, and they must have prepared and presented your claim with professionalism.

156. Remember, you must keep an eye on the website to keep abreast of the radical changes in funding arrangements which are likely to come into effect in April 2013.

SECTION 9: WHO WILL PAY MY COMPENSATION IF I AM SUCCESSFUL, AND WHY?

WHY ISN'T THE PERSON WHO HURT ME PAYING MY DAMAGES?

157. It is exceptionally rare that the person (often a driver) or organisation (often your employer) responsible for your injury personally pays your compensation.

158. The requirements of compulsory insurance mean that almost immediately after a claim is notified to the insurance company it 'steps into the shoes' of the defendant, and 'takes over' the defence of the claim.

159. This is not always the case, because in some very rare circumstances, insurers 'avoid' providing 'indemnity' (i.e. cover) because their client has breached some term of the insurance contract between them. There are also special circumstances in which compensation is provided by a different legal entity, for example:

    (a) The Criminal Injuries Compensation Authority ('CICA') where the injury arises from a criminal act (**see the link of the website**);

    (b) The Motor Insurer's Bureau ('MIB'). This body deals with road traffic claims where the driver who was responsible for the accident was either uninsured or cannot be found (**see the link on the website**).

HOW SHOULD THE INJURED PERSON VIEW THE INSURER?

160. It is an obvious point, but worth making: the insurer did not hurt you. The job of the insurer, and the solicitor/barrister they may instruct to defend the claim, is to challenge your claim on fault/liability, and try to restrict the amount of your compensation. So, on the one hand, the insurer is your inevitable 'adversary' in the process, but on the other hand, it is vital to retain a professional relationship with them to promote the best settlement of your claim.

THE 'RESERVE'

161. Insurers make an early assessment of the potential value of a claim, and they select a 'reserve', which is the total likely cost to them of your damages, your costs, and their costs. It is important to the insurer (as they plan their

finances) that the total value of the claim does not exceed the reserve. Also, as the claim develops, the insurer will re-assess the reserve to reflect changing circumstances.

SECTION 10: WHAT AGGRAVATES INSURERS AND HOW IT CAN AFFECT YOU

162. In broad terms, insurers are aggravated by inflated claims, and late additions to a claim, which could undercut an otherwise good offer the insurer has made. Clearly, also, insurers are determined, as they should be, to prevent dishonest claims from succeeding.

ENTIRELY DISHONEST CLAIMS

163. There are some (mercifully few) claimants who bring entirely false claims, arising from accidents which did not happen, or were arranged. There are friends or family members in some cases who claim to have been injured in a genuine accident but were not, in fact, present. Both of those types of 'claimant' rightly run the risk of a very severe criminal sanction, including being imprisoned.

DISHONESTY WITHIN A GOOD CLAIM

164. Insurers must also 'root out' dishonest or inflated claims in cases where there is a genuine injury. No insurer should have to pay compensation for claims which have been invented or badly exaggerated.

165. As the system is 'adversarial', there is an inevitable measure of tension between the parties. A person who has a poor work history before the accident will (on the face of it) find it very hard to persuade the insurer, or the judge, that he was likely to remain in unbroken employment, or gain repeated promotions but for the accident. A claim made on that basis is very likely to spur the defendant to investigate the claimant's work history in great detail (e.g. personnel records) and to scrutinise any Department of Work and Pensions ('DWP' **see the link on the website**) records (i.e. state benefits), and to obtain surveillance video footage to assess the claimant's capabilities and restrictions.

166. Once again, the key point is to remember that the claimant has to 'prove' the claims, and to do so requires sensible, credible evidence from him, and/or from former colleagues, or others who can provide persuasive evidence.

A NEW CLAIM MADE AT THE END OF THE PROCESS

167. The insurer will be aggravated by a claim which looks modest but then, at the last minute, after some frantic work on the claimant's side, results in a final Schedule of Loss, the document which summarises your claim, (see **section 17**) which is much higher than ever previously presented, and/or includes new claims, never before mentioned.

168. That sort of change can interfere with the insurer's ability to amend the 'reserve' in good time to make an offer to settle the claim. It may also make the insurer 'dig its heels in', and fight a claim which they might well have settled at a reasonable level.

169. An amended reserve may also require approval from someone more senior, which will inevitably cause irritation, resistance, and delay.

MAINTAINING THE RELATIONSHIP DESPITE YOUR DIFFERENCES

170. Although it is not immediately apparent, your aims and those of the insurer are often closer than you might think:
    (a) To maximise the prospects of the injured person returning to work, to earn as much money as possible (thereby reducing the insurer's exposure to a future loss claim).
    (b) To settle the claim;
    (c) To do so as early as possible, to restrict legal and other costs (e.g. ATE premiums can be extremely expensive, as well as escalating in stages during the claim);

171. Of course, in some cases, representatives on either side rub each other up the wrong way, and positions can easily become entrenched. A claimant may think the insurer is refusing an interim payment to 'wear him down' unfairly, and the insurer may think the claimant's side is inventing/prolonging claims to 'run up costs'.

172. Most cases can be run with firm, but courteous relationships between litigants. That is always preferable, because when parties fall out, they generally have to ask the Court to settle their differences – and any time the Court becomes involved, the result is less predictable.

173. The first and most important thing is to deal with the insurer as honestly as possible. Remember, suspicion generates resistance. It is worth reiterating that if you have told an expert that you cannot walk more than 100m, but as the months pass, you manage to walk a mile, and the defendant has footage of you doing so, they will think you are a person capable of exaggerating every aspect of your claim, and they will deal with your solicitor (and your claim) on that basis. Don't allow one sloppy inaccuracy to infect your whole claim.

174. The defendant often does not reveal any surveillance footage it may (typically in larger cases) have obtained until quite late in the case (see below). Typically, this is after you have signed your witness statement and/or an updated Schedule of Loss, setting out the restrictions and losses you are claiming, in a document you have certified as true.

175. It is also worth noting that one thing which impresses an insurer (and the Court for that matter) is a claimant who focuses on a return to work. Of course, you must not return before you are ready, and you might not manage a full, or even a gradual return. But, in general terms, making a genuine attempt to return to work is a simple way to communicate that you are trying to minimise the impact of the accident upon you.

SHOULD I ACCEPT AN OFFER OF REHABILITATION FROM THE INSURER?

176. This is an interesting and sometimes difficult issue. There is no doubt that good quality rehabilitation, in the right context, provided early on, can help to reverse the horrible downward spiral of: injury, pain, no money, no self-esteem, less chance of a return to work, etc.

    However, both parties can be resistant to it:

    (a) Some claimants feel a rehabilitation company appointed (and paid) by the defendant is really a 'spy in their camp' who will filter back information to the insurer which is detrimental to the claim;

    (b) Some defendants think that a claimant who does not accept rehabilitation is behaving unreasonably, and trying to maximise their claim instead of their recovery;

    (c) Similarly, defendants can feel that a claimant who does use the service, is really doing so to maximise their future earnings claim, for example, by deciding to undertake unrealistic, costly retraining (which they never would have considered before the accident).

177. Each case must be considered on its merits.

SECTION 11: WHY DID THE INSURER VIDEO ME?

178. Your lawyers have private access to you – they can meet and discuss the case with you at any time. The defendant is very unlikely ever to meet you to assess what type of person you are.

179. Indeed, both sides have private – or 'privileged' - access to their factual and expert witnesses, meaning that they can discuss the case with them in complete secrecy.

180. In a workplace claim, the insurer can try to glean an idea of who you are, what motivates you, etc., from your former boss or colleagues, and from the medical experts 'on their side' who have examined you.

181. In a road traffic accident ('RTA') case you will almost never know the defendant and it will be difficult for the insurer to get a feel for who you are, except by asking their own medical experts.

182. In a some larger cases, perhaps generally over £50,000 in value, and any case in which they are suspicious, the defendant is likely to supplement their knowledge of you by obtaining covert surveillance evidence. This involves employing a surveillance agency to film you, perhaps randomly, or when you are having a medical appointment with one of the defendant experts - because on that occasion you will be easier to find!

183. This can seem very intrusive, even sinister, but it more fairly reflects the fact that the defendant has very little evidence upon which to base their valuation of a claim. Also, they may 'hit the jackpot' if you are shown doing something you have categorically said you cannot do, or managing to do much more than you have professed. This reinforces the importance of telling your solicitor of significant improvements in your symptoms, which enable you to undertake more activities than before.

184. It is extremely awkward for your representatives if they are shown a DVD of you walking for 3 miles in no apparent pain, when you have at the same time (even on that very day) told a defendant expert you could only walk for a few hundred yards before suffering pain. The consequences can be widely felt:

(a) Your expert sees the footage, and feels 'let down' by your account to them (making him more likely to shift his ground in a joint discussion and joint report);

(b) Your representatives worry that the judge will lose faith in you at a trial, so that they have to lower their sights (and downgrade your expectations) in the claim – and possibly accept an offer which would otherwise appear much too low.

185. If there is a trial, you will be stressed by the thought that, at some point, you will be asked why you 'lied' to the expert, as opposing counsel tries to use one piece of clear inconsistency to ruin your credibility and turn the judge against each element of your claim.

WHAT YOU NEED TO KNOW ABOUT THE LAW IN PRACTICE

—
PART THREE
—

SECTION 12: INTRODUCTION TO EVIDENCE

186. There are broadly two types of evidence in injury litigation: factual evidence and expert evidence.

FACTUAL EVIDENCE – EVIDENCE OF EVENTS

187. Factual evidence (also known as 'lay' evidence, as in 'layperson') is simply evidence of facts and events given by individuals who have observed them at first hand.

188. Factual evidence is set out in writing in a 'witness statement', which the witness must sign to certify that the contents are true. At a trial, and with only very few exceptions, a person's entire factual evidence is contained in the statement, and he is only able to amplify the contents to a limited degree, by answering questions from his barrister (called 'examination in chief') before the defendant can ask its own questions ('cross-examination').

189. Given that the parties exchange their factual statements (usually) some months before the trial, there is an opportunity to consider the strengths and weaknesses of the evidence (and even to try to 'cure' weaknesses with further evidence, and seek permission to introduce it later than provided for by the Court). Generally, this is the point when the parties decide if, and how, to try to negotiate a settlement to the claim (**section 20 - 25**).

190. The content of your statement and that of other witnesses is therefore vital to the claim.

191. Quite apart from being truthful and internally consistent (i.e. not contradicting itself in different parts), each statement should be consistent with the other evidence (such as other witness statements and relevant documentation) or explain any inconsistencies which exist. However, in addition to those basic requirements, it is vital that the statement:
    (a) Expresses the evidence in the manner that the witness will use when answering questions, rather than being written in the solicitor's or barrister's style – which immediately looks and 'feels' artificial. Once the document is certified as true and accurate, it becomes the document of the witness just as if he had written it out and signed it, so it should be true (!) and be drafted in terms he would use and can understand;

(b) Communicates the facts clearly and fluently to the defendant and the judge. The easiest way to achieve this is to make it chronological, and to use frequent sub-headings to introduce different sections of the evidence.

192. Even a truthful statement that is badly prepared can have damaging consequences for the case. The statement can be incomplete in a crucial respect, or it might jump backwards and forwards in time so that the judge cannot understand how the facts link together. This is often the case when the 'author' tries to compile the statement in stages, without carefully reviewing what has previously been written. For example, each time the statement is updated, there are words like 'now' or 'recently' which mean nothing at all several years later, and confuse and annoy the judge, and make it very difficult for the witness to understand their own statement when giving evidence.

193. Also, in a complicated case with a long statement, it will be difficult for the judge to understand the important issues if he is presented with pages of unbroken text. The best statements are very often broken down into clear, sub-headed sections.

194. Some solicitors are excellent at compiling statements, others less so. Whoever prepares your statement, you should be prepared to help them as much as possible:

(a) Read the document very critically;

(b) Do not assume that it will be accurate just because a lawyer has prepared it;

(c) The statement is the foundation of your case and you must ensure that it is:

  (i) An history of events in your life, before and after the accident,

  (ii) Communicated in language that you would use if describing the events to someone who did not know you.

195. Remember the basics and insist that your statement is chronological, careful, comprehensive, consistent, and broken down into manageable sub-headed chunks. It is your statement and your claim!

EXPERT EVIDENCE - OPINIONS

196. Expert evidence is not evidence of fact, but evidence of opinion, from people trained in a specific discipline. Very simply put, expert evidence supplements the Court's knowledge with evidence in specialist fields in which judges (and lawyers) have no training. As a result, personal injury claims always involve expert opinion evidence, in the form of medical reports, describing the injury, providing a diagnosis, and prognosis.

197. Expert evidence is also often useful in difficult liability disputes, whether 'reconstructing' the events of a road accident, or commenting on a working practice. It can also be used to assist the Court:

    (a) to understand a person's care needs (a nursing or occupational therapist's report);

    (b) to appreciate the impact of the injury of the Claimant's career (an employment expert);

    (c) in assessing a case involving complex financial, typically business, losses (a forensic accountant).

198. It is important to realise that under the Civil Procedure Rules which govern how claims are made (which you can view on the **link on the website**), the Court has a duty to restrict expert evidence to that which is "reasonably required" to resolve the issues in dispute. Neither party should rush to instruct a host of experts unless and until such evidence is necessary.

THE POSITION AND IMPORTANCE OF THE EXPERT WITNESS

199. Expert witnesses have an "overriding duty to the Court" to provide their complete opinion on matters within their expertise. In other words, whilst their position is critical to the outcome of the case, they have a higher duty to inform the Court of their entire opinion even if it harms the position of the party instructing them.

200. In a liability dispute, whether in the workplace, or on the road, a negative opinion from an expert instructed on your behalf will be extremely detrimental, if not fatal to the claim, because it will make it very difficult for your representatives to 'certify' to the BTE/ATE insurer that your prospects of success are high enough to justify insuring you against the risk of losing (**section 8**).

201. In a valuation dispute, it is just as crucial that the expert provides authoritative, persuasive, supportive evidence. If your factual and expert evidence do not persuade the defendant to make a reasonable offer, then:
    (a) You are likely to receive a poor settlement offer;
    (b) If you have not persuaded the defendant, you may very well not persuade the Court either, so that your award will be low or you may lose your case entirely.

WHO WILL PAY FOR EXPERT REPORTS AND DOES IT MATTER?

202. The foundation of your claim will be:
    (a) your factual evidence, and that of witnesses;
    (b) the medical evidence of your injuries
    (c) (potentially) expert evidence concerning 'liability',
    (d) (and possibly) additional expert evidence concerning, for example, future care needs.

203. In cases in which 'liability' is denied, the defendant is very unlikely to have to pay for any 'liability' or 'medical reports' up front (i.e. before the case ends). That makes sense because if the defendant is successful, it ought not to have to pay any of the claimant's costs or expenses. Of course, those reports may be vital to the claim and, as discussed in **section 4**, you will need to know – in advance - whether your solicitor will pay for the necessary expert evidence.

204. In some cases, there may be a preliminary trial about liability (called a 'split trial' – because it 'splits' the 'fault' and valuation issues), especially if:
    (a) A claimant win would result in a very large claim, but
    (b) A defendant win would defeat the claim completely.

205. In both situations (liability denied, or possible split trial) it is vital that you know, early on, whether your representatives can find the appropriate expert and fund the report, or whether they are going to ask you to pay for such a report. You may want to approach several firms to find one which is prepared to pay for appropriate reports, or explain why they cannot do so.

206. In cases where liability is admitted, or partially admitted, it may well be the case that your solicitor can obtain an 'interim payment' for you from the defendant (**section 19**). This is exceptionally important because it will give you some much needed income. Some firms require that part of an interim payment is used to pay for expert reports. Once again, you may want to approach several firms to try to find one which is prepared to release all interim payments to you. You may still choose to be represented by a firm that cannot offer that funding, if you feel that they are the best firm for you, but it is vital to know in advance how interim payments will be used as the claim progresses.

207. The defendant will almost certainly not make voluntary interim payments of more than perhaps 50% – 60% of the value of even a liability-admitted claim. Therefore, where in a moderate sized claim (value about £50,000) if considerable sums are spent on expert reports, that will inevitably restrict the amount you can hope to receive to replace your income (and pay for necessities such as treatment).

208. If your solicitor does intend to spend an interim payment on expert reports, or other expenses (called 'disbursements'), you must consider whether that is detrimental to you and whether there are alternatives available. That is because the interim payment generally replaces your lost earnings and expenditure at a time when you will badly need funds.

209. The same applies later on, if and when you may ask the Court to order the defendant to make an interim payment. It will order a sum which is 'no more than a reasonable proportion' of the eventual claim, to avoid a situation where a defendant might 'overpay' and have to recover money from you after the claim finishes.

210. If your solicitor needs to use interim payments to pay for medical (and other) reports, there will be a great deal less of the interim payment for you.

211. You will need to consider whether that means you should consider looking for a replacement solicitor (**section 6 - 7**), who can 'foot the bill' for such reports, or whether you are happy with your present solicitors (and were made aware of this issue from the outset).

WHAT YOU NEED FROM AN EXPERT

212. It is critical that the experts selected to assist the Court are:

    (a) High quality, independent, and respected;

    (b) Possess precisely relevant expertise.

INSTRUCTING THE EXPERT: GETTING IT RIGHT

213. Your solicitor should instruct an expert who possesses the necessary professionalism and specialist knowledge. You should press him to discuss this issue with you (if you choose to become involved) and if necessary your barrister, when making the selection. You need to know, in advance, that your solicitor will select the correct expert and fund the reports needed to construct your claim.

214. If for any reason your solicitor is unsure about the instruction, ask him to obtain an 'example' report from the expert (with the names deleted, or as lawyers say 'redacted') so that he can see the expert's typical style and thoroughness, and ensure that (for example):

    (a) He reviews the medical notes carefully;

    (b) He provides a clear balanced opinion;

    (c) He explains reasons for the opinions he expresses.

215. This can be crucial where your solicitor is unfamiliar with the expert, or with the area of expertise. No reasonable expert should object to sending such an example of his medico-legal work.

216. Also, if you are interested, there is no reason why you should not consider the example report as well, and give your opinions.

SECTION 13: PITFALLS WITH EXPERT EVIDENCE

ONE CHANCE TO SELECT THE RIGHT EXPERT

217. The Court (understandably) hates to think that you or the insurer will 'shop around' until you find a professional opinion to suit your case. It has therefore developed a rule that if either of you have ever obtained an expert report for your claim (i.e. under the Court Rules), but then decide to rely upon another report in the same discipline, you will almost always have to give the first report to the other side (who is permitted to refer to it at trial).

218. You can immediately see that it is vital to choose the correct expert first time around, and to provide that expert with every relevant piece of evidence.

219. A further reason for getting it right first time is because if the defendant obtains a report which agrees with your first expert, then there may be a worrying balance in the evidence 'against you', putting considerable pressure on your second expert. So you can also see that any second expert must be as authoritative as possible on the issues in dispute.

220. It is also worth noting that the presence of two opinions which support the defendant's arguments will also exert pressure on your lawyers when they come to consider the prospects that you will succeed to establish fault (where the report concerns 'liability') or beat an offer (where the report concerns valuation of the claim).

CAN YOU ALWAYS 'SWAP' EXPERTS IF YOU GIVE THE DEFENDANT THE FIRST REPORT?

221. No! You will have to provide careful, sensible reasons for wanting to change expert. These might be that:
    (a) The expert has done his job poorly (perhaps failing to read relevant notes, missing important points, etc), or
    (b) He was not sufficiently 'expert' in the field in which he offered an opinion (explained in the next sub-section).

222. One reason it is vital to be sure that your reasons are persuasive is because if your lawyer criticises expert 1 in an attempt to swap to expert 2, but fails to convince the Court, the defendant may seize on your own criticisms of

expert 1 as the claim progresses. So it cannot be emphasised enough that 'your side' must select experts with great care from the start.

223. It is also important to realise that the later in a claim you try to change expert, the worse your prospects of being permitted to do so. Generally this is because the case will be nearer to its conclusion, so that a change may result in a great deal of wasted costs, and may derail a timetable leading to the trial – something to which the Court is understandably resistant.

THE WRONG EXPERT

224. If, for example, you have a spinal injury, the most appropriate expert is probably a spinal surgeon, or orthopaedic surgeon with a special interest in spinal surgery. If one side instructs someone whose day to day practice is spinal surgery and the other party instructs an A&E consultant (even an excellent one), there is already an imbalance of expertise. The spinal surgeon may have more command of the narrow field in question, be more familiar with the studies and journals concerned with spinal practice, and be effortlessly authoritative in his report, and then in the witness box.

225. If this happens to you, then unless the respective opinions are very similar, it may well be necessary to consider seeking permission to instruct a suitably skilled replacement expert. You must be aware that as well as needing to persuade the Court to permit such a change, 'your side' is going to have to pay for the second opinion (after all the defendant did not choose the wrong expert for you). That may cause tension between you and your solicitor – but it needs to be dealt with as soon as the problem arises.

THE LAZY EXPERT

226. It is vital that your expert takes his job seriously and professionally. Experts are generally well rewarded for medico-legal reports, and it is only reasonable that they should see your claim as just as important as any other aspect of their work. You should not be made to feel as if your claim is an irritating inconvenience at the end of a busy working day in hospital.

227. Your representatives should never disclose a medical report unless you have seen it and provided your comments (perhaps to clarify a misunderstanding, or correct simple errors). You and your representatives ought not to have

to point out errors and omissions (e.g. some missing medical notes), but this does often happen where the expert has not devoted enough time or care to the report. It is extremely frustrating, time-consuming, and creates awkwardness between the expert and his instructing party, reinforcing the need to select a high quality expert from the start.

228. It is even worse to see an expert struggling to maintain consistency in their opinion when answering (perfectly reasonable) tough questions from the defendant, or worse still, being forced to change their initial opinion because they missed important information.

229. The worst scenario is when an expert effectively capitulates, or changes their opinion on a crucial issue. This might be because they were wrong in the first place, but it can also occur when they have given an unrealistic initial opinion and/or (worse still) when they feel embarrassed by the thought of being cross-examined at trial. This is mercifully rare, but it can happen, and have dire effects on the claim.

COLLATING THE MEDICAL RECORDS

230. This is an absolutely critical aspect of the case. The experts on both sides must have all of you medical records (including all treatment records), in order to provide a professional and reliable opinion. They will also want to see DWP (i.e. benefits) documentation, and occupational health records, as these become available.

231. It is often very difficult for the solicitor to obtain records from many different sources exactly when they are needed (especially because notes of your treatment will be 'ongoing').

232. The first thing is to tell your solicitor about all the medical professionals you have seen: hospitals attended, GP details, physiotherapists, chiropractors, etc. Don't forget to mention if you have had x-rays and MRI scans, etc.

233. Most people never see their medical notes until they have an injury claim. At that point, as you will see, the experts and lawyers pore over every entry, to support their arguments.

234. The records sometimes contain important information which jogs your memory, or information that you cannot remember. The person writing

down information, whether your GP, a locum (i.e. stand-in) GP, a physiotherapist, or a busy A&E doctor will have tried to record what you tell them, because that was vital information to assess and treat you at the time. However, they may occasionally have made a mistake, misunderstood something you told them, or misplaced emphasis.

235. Both because it is vital that your solicitors have obtained your complete notes, and because of the possibility of errors in those notes (which should be addressed as soon as possible) it may, in a serious case, be sensible to ask your solicitor for your own copy of the records which have been sent to the experts. This may seem like 'overkill', and in many cases it will not be necessary. But in a difficult case in which it seems likely that the notes will be important, you may decide that it would be sensible to see your medical notes.

236. Later on, in **section 17**, the importance of contemporary documents is explained. For now, it is worth emphasising that if you see any significant errors in your notes, or other documents written down (or compiled on computer) by someone else, you should raise the issue straight away. That way, your solicitor can alert the defendant to the error before it assumes significance in the case (as well as raising it with the 'author' if that is sensible in the circumstances). As you can imagine, it is always less satisfactory to complain about the accuracy of a note after an expert or other witness has placed reliance upon it.

237. One of the potential difficulties when a solicitor obtains a medical report through a medical agency (which often happens when you are based a long way from the solicitor's office) is that the agency itself obtains the medical records (rather than your solicitor doing so). This can be convenient, and some agencies are professional and efficient, but it prevents your solicitor having 'control over' the collation of records. Sometimes this results in medical records becoming fragmented, or not being updated, so that the expert does not see all of the important documents, scans, x-rays etc, when providing the opinion.

238. Often the best way to manage medical records is by separating them into (paginated) chronological sections, reflecting the different hospitals, GP notes, medical treatment notes, therapy notes (e.g. physiotherapy). This may not be necessary in every case, but it is certainly worth considering in any

case where there has been a considerable amount of medical treatment, over more than a year or so.

239. It can be extremely dangerous for your expert to express a very strident opinion before seeing all of the notes. The expert can later look foolish, or just plain wrong, when some previously unseen notes become available. Even if the expert changes opinion, in keeping with the new notes, there remains a sense (and a judge might later feel) that he should not have offered such a strong opinion before seeing relevant material. There are also cases in which the expert may not know that there are missing notes (the expert does not know every physiotherapist, etc., you might have seen), but that will not stop the 'other side' from criticising the expert if he has to change opinion at a later stage.

DEALING WITH QUESTIONS BY ANOTHER PARTY

240. The Court Rules (very sensibly) permit a party to pose questions to clarify an expert's report.

241. When any party poses questions to an expert to clarify his opinion, they do so to improve their position, usually by trying to persuade the expert that one or more aspects of the opinion are incorrect (perhaps by drawing his attention to a specific piece of evidence, often a medical note, which they do not has been taken into account). That is an entirely legitimate part of the process.

242. It is also legitimate for your representatives to discuss any questions posed to your expert by another party before they are answered, or to request draft answers and a discussion with the expert before they are finalised. (The defendant can and should do exactly the same with their own experts).

243. Some experts remain very 'old school' and are very reluctant to discuss their evidence in this way. However, as long as your lawyers carefully acknowledge that the Court is only interested in the expert's entire opinion it is entirely permissible to explore the expert's reasoning with him before the answers are finalised.

TRYING TO ENSURE THAT THE JOINT EXPERT REPORT DOES NOT GO PEAR-SHAPED

244. The Court almost always orders discussions between experts in the same discipline to produce a joint report. The aim of the process, and the joint report, is to clarify the areas and extent of agreement between the experts and, crucially, to try to narrow (or even eliminate) the areas on which they disagree.

245. That discussion takes place privately, and neither party ought to interfere in the process once discussions have begun.

246. Of course, the very nature of the discussion means that one or other party could be extremely disappointed by the outcome. The worst situation for one or other side is when 'their' expert completely changes his opinion following a formal discussion with the other side's expert. This can happen in any case, but it is far less likely where the experts are professional and have been provided with all relevant material when reaching their original opinion.

247. Indeed, 'cracks' most often seem to appear in an expert's opinion in the joint report when one expert:
    (a) Has given an overly supportive opinion in the first place;
    (b) Is embarrassed by an error in the original report, and does not relish being cross-examined at trial;
    (c) Was not provided with complete instructions and/or medical notes when finalising the original report (missing something relevant and making them vulnerable to persuasion).

248. In rare cases, one expert is completely persuaded by (and 'to') the opinion of the other party's expert, so that the 'joint report' expresses a single opinion ("we agree that……..."). That effectively ruins that party's case, unless:
    (a) Another expert can be found to express a supportive opinion, and
    (b) Permission can be obtained to rely upon a further expert report at so late a stage in the case.

249. As explained above, it is increasingly difficult to change experts as the claim progresses.

250. There can also be a feeling from the 'joint report' that the more 'generalist' expert has been 'outgunned' by the more specialist expert, and again there may be a suspicion that the generalist might not want to undergo cross-examination at trial, knowing that someone with more command of their subject will also be addressed by the Court.

MAKING SURE THE EXPERT IS PREPARED FOR THE JOINT REPORT

251. One way to improve the outcome of a joint report is to ensure that the expert is thoroughly prepared. Often experts are surgeons in active NHS practice, and their litigation work is conducted after a busy and stressful day. For that reason, it is sensible to do what you can, within the rules, to assist in the run up to the joint discussion:

   (a) You might ask your solicitor if he and your barrister (and you if you want) can discuss the claim with the barrister and expert before the joint report – it never hurts to remind the expert of the issues on which his opinion have been provided before a discussion. Having a conference will mean he will probably prepare thoroughly, and then have a fresher recollection of the case during the joint discussion;

   (b) You might ask your solicitor to provide a neutral agenda for the discussion, to make sure the expert covers all the areas you need to be covered. This can be sent to the defendant for agreement and can often be uncontroversial. This will ensure, especially in a complicated case, that the parties do not have to waste weeks and weeks posing questions after the joint report just to make sure all necessary areas are discussed;

   (c) If your representatives are worried that the expert might miss important points which have assisted his reasoning in the original report, or weak points in the other party's reasoning, they may choose to provide the expert with notes for his use only, helping to remind him of those issues. Again, your side must keep in mind appropriate professional boundaries between advocates and experts, and be sensitive to the style of your expert (who might not like such 'intrusion'), but there is nothing wrong with reminding trying to ensure that the expert does express his complete opinion.

SECTION 14: WHAT IS 'CAUSATION' AND WHY DOES IT MATTER?

PRELIMINARY POINTS – (I) THE BURDEN OF PROOF

252. When you bring a claim, you have to demonstrate that the person you are suing was responsible for the accident, and was responsible for your injuries and financial losses. Put into legal jargon, you have the 'burden of proof'.

253. In some situations, that 'burden' switches to the defendant. So, for example, if the defendant alleges that you were in part to blame for an accident, or (as explained below) that your conduct at some time after the accident caused some of your losses, it has the burden of proving those allegations.

254. In many cases, these issues are straightforward, and you will not have to think about them. However, it is always worth remembering in general terms who has to prove what.

PRELIMINARY POINTS – (II) THE STANDARD OF PROOF

255. Where a party has the 'burden' of proving something in a claim, such as the defendant's driving, or an employer's failure to provide equipment, caused the accident, he only has to prove that 'it was more likely than not' to be the case. Lawyers refer to it as proving something on 'a balance of probability'. Some people think of the test in very simple terms as proving something was 51% likely to happen (ie just over the 50% balance).

256. You can see that it is a much lower level of 'proof' than is required in a criminal case, where the prosecution has to prove its case against a criminal defendant 'beyond a reasonable doubt'.

CAUSATION – WHAT CAUSED THAT TO HAPPEN?

257. As I discussed in **section 2**, you are entitled to recover damages for the injuries and losses which were caused by the accident you suffered. That sounds very simple, and in the vast majority of cases, it is simple. So, in a typical minor road accident claim, when one person (the defendant) drives his car into the rear of a car in front of him, injuring the driver (the claimant) the losses may be:

(a) Neck pain for 4 weeks;

(b) Modest vehicle damage;

(c) A few days off work;

(d) Three sessions of physiotherapy;

(e) Travel/parking costs for physiotherapy.

258. It ought to be quick and straightforward to 'prove' that it was 'more likely than not' that the defendant 'caused' the accident, the injury, and the financial losses.

259. Of course, many cases concern more complicated events, both relating to the accident and to the losses. Take, for example, a situation in which a man is unable to return to work for six months because of his injuries. He claims six months earnings loss, which on the face of it seems a very easy claim to prove. But what if he was likely to be sacked or made redundant anyway (for reasons unrelated to the accident), or if his employer went into liquidation during that period?

260. If he was not going to be able to earn his wages for some of that period regardless of the accident, then the accident did not cause that loss.

261. Given that you need to 'prove' that it is 'more likely than not' that each of the losses you are claiming was 'caused' by the defendant, it is always important to keep your eye on 'cause and effect'. Lawyers have another way of asking the same question about each of elements of a claim: "what, but for (meaning 'in the absence of') the accident, was likely to have happened in the future?"

262. As you can see, because the claims (e.g. lost earnings) concern events (going to work and being paid) which would have happened after the date of the accident if the accident had not happened, there is very often scope to argue that the future may have been different (sacking, liquidation, etc).

263. Lawyers and their clients in injury claims have to focus upon proving, 'on a balance of probability', what the future would have been if the injury had not happened, and what the future now holds (given the impact of the accident injuries).

264. At every stage of the claim, from establishing fault for your accident, to proving the losses which you have suffered, your lawyers, and you, will keep coming back to the issue of causation. In fact, lawyers have another phrase which reflects what they are trying to achieve: 'the chain of causation'. This really does mean a 'chain' - with the 'accident' at one end, and the losses caused by the accident all connected together.

265. You might like to think of a 'chain' for each element of your claim, so that you can keep thinking of how to establish the 'links' between the accident and the losses which are said to have resulted.

266. In what follows, I am only intending to provide some examples of the issues you may encounter because each person's circumstances and claims are unique. You will see that the chain of causation can be broken, and that even if it is not broken, there are circumstances in which claims can still be reduced.

EXAMPLES OF CAUSATION - (I) LIABILITY

267. In one old case, a man was sent home by an A&E doctor who had failed to diagnose that he was suffering from arsenic poisoning. The man died and his widow sued the hospital. The hospital admitted that the doctor was negligent for failing to diagnose arsenic poisoning, but successfully argued that his negligence had caused no loss. By the time he saw the doctor, it was too late to administer the antidote for the poisoning so that the man would have died anyway.

268. Using the chain of causation analogy, the fact that he could not be cured anyway, broke the chain between the negligent diagnosis and the losses suffered by his widow. She would have suffered those same losses even if the correct diagnosis had been made and the best possible treatment given to her husband. In a nutshell, the negligence did not cause any loss.

EXAMPLES OF CAUSATION - (II) BREAKING THE CHAIN OF CAUSATION

269. In relation to valuation, there are many examples of claims which are cut short by a completely unrelated event. In one case, a Mr McKew (who had been caused a knee injury by the admitted negligence of the defendant) visited a property with his family. He knew that as a result of his earlier

accident his knee was likely to give way suddenly and without warning. Nevertheless, when he left the property, Mr McKew chose to use a very steep stairway, which did not have a handrail, and to walk close to his child instead of other adult family members (who might have been able to help him if his leg gave way). His leg did give way and he suffered serious injuries. In that case the Court decided that Mr McKew's conduct was so unreasonable that it broke the chain of causation. That meant that he could not recover the losses caused by his fall from the person who had originally injured his knee.

EXAMPLES OF CAUSATION - (III) CONTRIBUTORY FAULT

270. As you have just seen, the law sometimes judges that a person's actions are so unreasonable that they break the chain of causation. That is not the only outcome where an injured person has suffered a second accident or injury in his day to day life. In a recent case, a Mr Spencer suffered an amputation as a result of a negligently caused injury. As a result, he wore a prosthetic leg, and had walking sticks to help him. Mr Spencer was able to drive an automatic car when his leg was not attached, and usually placed it on the rear seat behind him. One day, at a petrol station, he left his car without his leg or his sticks. He filled his car, then hopped back towards the driver's door to hoot for the attendant to come and take his payment. Unfortunately, as he returned, Mr Spencer tripped on an uneven manhole cover, fell and suffered further injuries which confined him permanently to a wheelchair.

271. The Court decided that Mr Spencer's actions, unlike those of Mr McKew, were not so unreasonable as to break the chain of causation, linking his original injury (and amputation) to his fall. However, it decided that he had not acted with reasonable care, so that he bore some contributory fault (assessed at one third or 33%) for the additional injuries.

PUTTING THE CLAIM TOGETHER

—
PART FOUR
—

SECTION 15: HOW YOU SHOULD APPROACH THE CLAIM

FIRST CONTACT: START ON THE RIGHT FOOT

272. The injured person is very likely to provide the central factual evidence to prove who caused the accident/injury (the 'liability' issue) and what losses have been suffered (the 'valuation' or 'quantum' issue). The first contact with the solicitor is very likely to be by telephone, and you should remember that solicitors keep notes of such discussions (called 'attendance notes'), to help remind them about it afterwards.

273. It is very importnat to be as careful and accurate as possible, from the first contact, because what you say may well be communicated to the defendant (e.g. in letters). If there are inconsistencies or inaccuracies, the defence insurer may be encouraged to think that your evidence can be undermined, which may make it (understandably) suspicious. If it spots other inconsistencies, relating to liability, or valuation issues, it may deal with the case in a different manner (for example, withholding interim payments).

RECOGNISE THE IMPORTANCE OF ORIGINAL DOCUMENTS

274. The defence insurer, and later the Court, will scrutinise the original, contemporary documents in a case very carefully. Where there is opposing evidence from witnesses (often trying to justify their own position) there are often very strong clues as to who is correct, contained in documentation which was created immediately after the accident.

275. For example, in a disputed liability case, this might be the first comments of the two drivers recorded in a Police Accident Report; or the content of a workplace incident report; or a Heath and Safety Executive ('HSE') RIDDOR report (Report of Injury, Disease and Dangerous Occurrence). **(see the link on the website)**.

276. In many cases, lawyers pore over GP records and other medical notes to see whether there are damaging inconsistencies in the claimant's accounts:

    (a) Of the accident at the scene (police and/or ambulance staff notes);

    (b) At Accident and Emergency (hospital staff notes);

(c) To the surgeons (often some days later);

(d) Those providing treatment/therapies (physiotherapists etc.);

(e) Those assessing benefit claims (your DWP records will all be available for scrutiny – and are often highly detailed).

277. Those documents become a crucial part of the fabric of your claim. There is no reason to be too worried about them, providing you recognise the importance of trying to give accurate information at all times. To reiterate the point made in **section 13**, if there are errors in such documents, you should point them out straight away to your solicitor.

IS THERE ANYTHING ELSE I SHOULD DO?

278. Yes - help your legal team! If you feel able to assist, do not let the claim go on around you. Be central to it.

279. You may take pride and satisfaction in seeing the claim take shape, and being sensibly put together, and you can help the process by answering questions and dealing with issues – so that the areas in dispute between the parties continually narrow. That is also likely to enhance the prospects a reasonable settlement being achieved.

SECTION 16: ELEMENTS OF THE CLAIM

There are checklists based upon the contents on this section at the end of the guide

LIABILITY

280. As far as liability (the 'fault issue') is concerned, whatever the nature of your accident:

   (a) Write down an account as soon as you can;

   (b) If possible, take several photos immediately after any accident, to illustrate what happened, the position of vehicles, a piece of dangerous equipment, etc. (use your phone or keep a disposable camera in your glove-box);

   (c) Consider whether anyone else might be able to provide information about the accident;

   (d) Consider whether someone could provide evidence in a broader context (eg in a workplace claim) on issues relating to training, or equipment;

   (e) Also, in a workplace claim, try to note down names and addresses of any individuals who leave the defendant's employment who might be able to provide relevant evidence concerning liability issues, or valuation issues (eg your reputation, opportunities for promotion, etc.). Such individuals may feel less 'constrained' about giving evidence relating to their former workplace after they have left;

   (f) Consider in as balanced a way as you can whether you might have done anything wrong yourself, which might have contributed to your injury.

VALUATION OF YOUR CLAIM: 'QUANTUM'

281. As far as quantum is concerned, keep in mind the key areas of your likely claim, typically: earnings, personal care, and assistance with heavier domestic tasks.

LOSS OF EARNINGS OR INCOME

282. As regards earnings, there is a great deal you can do. Keep payslips, tax records, accounts, order books – anything which will help to show how you have earned your living both before and after the accident. Consider

realistically (not pessimistically) what the future probably held if the accident had not happened:

(a) Is your employer still trading?

(b) Would you still have the same job?

(c) Would you have had a pay rise?

(d) Might you have had a promotion. If so:-

   (i) Who was your competition?

   (ii) Why were you 'better'?

   (iii) Did you have periodic appraisals which would show how well you were doing?

   (iv) Who got the promotion?

(e) were you receiving any valuable employment benefits, apart from wages, which are now lost: e.g. health insurance, use of vehicle, telephone;

(f) If the employer has gone into liquidation, what would you then have done if you had not been injured?

(g) What were your chances of finding further work, and at what wage, and when, and where?

(h) Might there have been increased or reduced travel costs in further work?

(i) What qualifications did you have before the accident?

(j) Can you still use any of those qualifications, or if not, is that because of the accident, or for some other reason?

(k) What can you manage now?

(l) Can you re-train in a field you know?

(m) How long would re-training take, what would it cost, what is the rate of successful completion (something the college or provider should tell you), and what proportion of successful candidates find work?

(n) Do you know what opportunities there may be?

(o) Could you re-train in a new field altogether?

(p) How long would re-training take, what would it cost, what is the rate of successful completion (again, something the college or provider should tell you), and what proportion of successful candidates find work in that field?

(q) Do you know what opportunities there may be?

(r) What could you do if you did not pass the re-training course/exams?

283. If, prior to the accident, you ran your own business, rather than being an employee, you will have to consider slightly different questions, bearing in mind all the time that you will be challenged on every aspect of the claim you advance. Be realistic and be as accurate as possible - but do not be a pessimist.

284. It is vital to persuade the insurers, and if necessary the judge, about your earnings, and prospects of pay increases or promotion. Insurers are likely to argue that all such suggestions are 'speculative' because they had not yet happened. Of course they are, as everything in the future is by definition speculative! Your job, with your advisers, is to provide evidence (your own, colleagues, etc.) which 'builds likelihood' (it was probably going to happen) in the place of speculation (there was a chance it might have happened).

EXPERT EVIDENCE TO ASSESS EFFECTS OF THE ACCIDENT ON INCOME

285. In the same way that the parties involve medical experts, they may also involve two types of expert to provide the Court with evidence about the impact of the accident upon your earnings. The first is the expert accountant (also called a forensic accountant) to assist in assessing complicated wage (and pension) losses, and lost business profits.

286. These experts can be extremely important in helping the lawyers to understand and explain the way in which a business ran before the accident, and as far as possible, what the future held. Their expertise can also make it far more economical for them (as opposed to the lawyers) to compile evidence of earnings loss or loss of and profit in complicated cases.

287. The second is an employment expert. These experts can be extremely valuable providing they really have expertise which neither the parties (having conducted reasonable research) nor the Court (with a wealth of experience of injury claims) possess. In general terms, judges are resistant to permit the involvement of employment experts. They have been known to comment that the material provided in the report could have been found on the internet, that the cost of the expert evidence is not proportionate to the issues involved, or that the analysis was not sufficiently expert to assist.

288. My experience is that providing they are carefully chosen and instructed, employment experts can provide extremely important evidence which the Court does find of considerable value – in the right case.

PERSONAL CARE

289. Following many injuries the injured person needs, and receives, personal 'care' from others, usually close family members. The nature and duration of such care varies in every case. A simple example might be a person who has difficulty bathing or dressing for a short period after an accident. A more complicated example could be intensive day and night time care, very similar to nursing care, which might last for many months or even years.

290. The law permits you to recover the value of such care, on the basis that at the end of your claim you will recompense the people who provided the care. The present hourly rate allowed is generally about £7.

291. It is sensible, but not essential, for someone to keep a record (perhaps weekly) of the sort of personal care provided to you (noting particularly any unsocial hours). This is more important in a case of serious injury, where the past pattern of family-provided care may be replaced in the future by paid care, which is compensated at a significantly higher rate.

292. If, instead of having care provided by family members or friends, an injured person is able to pay for such care themselves, then he will be able to recover the reasonable commercial costs.

293. In some cases, there are also legitimate claims for the care that the injured person was providing, or would have provided, to some other person (usually a close family member) if the accident had not happened.

DOMESTIC ASSISTANCE

294. The law also permits compensation in relation to tasks (such as household chores, DIY, gardening, etc.) which you would have undertaken if the accident had not happened. Typical examples are:
   (a) Cleaning;
   (b) Vacuuming;
   (c) Laundry and ironing;

(d) Cooking;

(e) Gardening;

(f) DIY/decorating;

(g) Window cleaning;

(h) Shopping;

(i) Vehicle maintenance / cleaning.

295. Each case and each person is different, and the evidence (in witness statements and the medical evidence) must support those claims, by persuading the insurer, and possibly the Court, that:

(a) The claimant used to undertake such tasks;

(b) But for the accident, he would have undertaken them in the future

(c) He cannot now manage them;

(d) There is no sensible way to re-distribute domestic tasks to reduce the need for someone else (whether a family member, friend, or paid 'outsider') to assist.

296. Therefore, for each of those tasks it is helpful if you, or someone on your behalf, can describe to your solicitor (even in a 'stream-of-consciousness' email, if that is easiest, which he can then fashion into a witness statement):

(a) Who used to undertake each task before the accident, how frequently, for how long, and who does it now, and why;

(b) If you were excellent at DIY or gardening etc., say so, and provide 'before photos' of work you had done, which demonstrate your pre-accident capabilities, which will help you to recover the cost of that work being undertaken professionally in the future;

(c) Think as broadly as you can – it may be that you have not yet owned a home with a garden, or a house (or a home you were responsible for), but try to explain your aptitudes, and what you expected would have happened, and when, if you had not been injured. Remember, you are simply trying to give a comprehensive picture of the likely impact of the accident upon you.

OTHER POTENTIAL CLAIMS

297. Also, when considering the effects of your injuries upon your life, it is important on the one hand not to miss important claims, whilst on the other hand to be sensible and realistic about whether the accident has actually caused a loss. Some further examples of relevant questions might be:

   (a) Will you need any extra equipment or furniture in your home?

   (b) Do you need an automatic vehicle?

   (c) Do you need an adapted vehicle?

   (d) Are you likely to incur additional travel costs?

   (e) Will conventional holidays be possible? If not, how can you be provided with holidays, and what additional costs might there be?

298. By considering these matters, and providing information about them, and any other issues relevant to your circumstances, you will be:

   (a) Helping to formulate each claim;

   (b) Providing evidence to support the claims;

   (c) Enabling the insurer, if necessary, to adjust the reserve.

SECTION 17: THE KEY LITIGATION DOCUMENTS

299. The importance of contemporary documents has been discussed previously (**section 15**). Now we come to the documents which must be created as a part of the claim.

LETTER OF CLAIM

300. The first is the letter of claim. This sets out basic information (your name, national insurance number, date of accident, etc.), gives a factual account of the accident, explains the legal basis of your claim, including which duties are alleged to have been broken, and requests certain documents from the defendant to enable you to consider your legal position in greater detail.

301. It goes without saying that it is critical that the factual account of the accident is accurate. In all but the most obvious cases (such as a rear end collision) you should ask to see the letter of claim before it is sent.

302. If there are inaccuracies in the letter, then the defendant will understandably raise these during the litigation (as well as any other inconsistencies). An accumulation of such inaccuracies may lead you to have to concede a deduction from the 100% value of the claim when trying to reach a settlement, because they have increased the risk that you might not persuade the Court that the defendant was (completely or partially) at fault for the accident. It is incredibly annoying to encounter situations where avoidable mistakes have been made which result in a person having to concede some proportion, or a greater portion, of their claim. It is critical that the facts communicated to the Defendant are clear and accurate.

303. A simple example is a tripping accident. A person who breaks their ankle as a result of a fall which they allege was caused by a bad highway defect has to prove (in general terms) that:

    (a) There was a defect present precisely where the accident took place;

    (b) The defect amounted to a danger;

    (c) The defect identified by the injured person caused the accident (i.e. it was not caused merely by the injured person tripping over his feet, or by a less serious defect nearby).

    (NB these are not the only issues in a tripping claim, and I use them merely to illustrate the point at hand concerning documentation).

304. It may be surprising to hear that some claims of this nature fail at trial because there are inconsistencies in the description of the location, and of the nature of the fall itself, recorded in the contemporary documents, and later in the letter of claim, and the 'Particulars of Claim' (discussed in the next section). There can also be inconsistencies between the 'mechanism of the accident' described by the injured person and the actual nature of the injury diagnosed by the medical expert.

305. In most cases, these issues are not problematic, but they can be important, and can significantly affect the way the claim progresses (and ends). It is therefore important to pay attention to the content of the letter of claim.

THE CLAIM FORM

306. The 'claim itself' (by which I mean 'court proceedings') is commenced by the 'issue' of a 'Claim Form'. This document contains certain important basic information: it names the parties involved; it describes the accident in a sentence or two, giving its date; it is stamped with the date on which the claim was issued.

307. The last point is important because it 'stops the clock'. A person injured by the negligence of another party (i.e. a person, an employer, etc.) generally has three years to 'issue' a claim. There is a host of provisions which can alter that basic rule, but in the majority of cases the relevant period allowed (called the 'limitation period') is three years from the accident.

PARTICULARS OF CLAIM

308. The 'Particulars of Claim' is the document which sets out the claim in greater detail – giving 'particulars' (simply meaning 'details') in a formal legal document (often mirroring the facts in the letter of claim) of:

    (a) The facts which are alleged to give rise to the claim;

    (b) The identity of the defendant who/which is blamed for causing the accident;

    (c) The legal principles upon which the claim is founded (usually the law of negligence, or a duty set out in an Act of Parliament (also known as a 'statute'), or 'Regulations', which have been made under the authority of a statute);

(d) The way in which the facts and legal principles relate to one another (this is the critical part of the document which sets out why the breaches of duty caused the injury);

(e) The nature of the injury, with some details, and reference to the supporting medical evidence;

(f) The fact that financial losses have been caused by the injury, and reference to the 'Schedule of Loss', which will set out the losses claimed to date.

SCHEDULE OF LOSS

309. The last of the three crucial court documents which must be sent to (or as lawyers say 'served on') the defendant is the Schedule of Loss. This sets out the financial losses which you have suffered to date, for example, lost earnings, care, domestic assistance, medication, transport costs, etc.

310. In a simple case, the Schedule may be able, even at this early stage, to set out all of your financial losses, because they have come to an end. In others, the Schedule may touch on the potential future claims, which will depend upon whether your recovery is complete or leaves you with restrictions in your ability to work, or daily activities. In very serious cases, even if the claim is issued close to the three year time limit, it may be that there is a great deal more medical (and other expert) evidence to obtain in order to quantify the long term claims.

A REQUIREMENT OF THE KEY LITIGATION DOCUMENTS - THE STATEMENT OF TRUTH

311. One of the most important features of the documents which have to be served on the defendant is that each of them must contain a 'statement of truth'. That is simply certification by you personally (or your lawyer, with your specific authorisation) that the facts in the document are true. A statement of truth simply states "I believe that the facts in this document are true".

312. It cannot be emphasised enough that any document you certify is thereafter considered your document (whoever drafted it). If something in any such document later proves to have been untrue or inaccurate at the time it was signed, that will make the insurers suspicious of you (and less likely to settle the claim, or at least to settle it at a level you had expected).

313. It can lead the insurer to consider that the accumulated inaccuracies, or inconsistencies, in the contemporary and court documents are such that the claim should be defended on liability, or on certain aspects of your claim. It may also make the insurer feel confident that only lower offers need to be made to provide them with reasonable 'costs protection' if there is a trial (**section 22, 23, and 26**).

314. Also, if the defendant can identify a number of 'inaccurate' or 'untrue' statements that you have certified as true, it is very likely that those will harm the way a judge would view your evidence at a trial – because it suggests you were either deliberately or carelessly signing an inaccurate or untrue document. Remember that although your case is very unlikely to 'go to court', in order to avoid circumstances in which your side is not ready to deal with all of the relevant issues in dispute, it must be prepared as if it would end in a trial.

315. Such inaccuracies in the evidence are bound to impact on the defendant's perception of you when considering settlement terms, and a judge's perception of you at a trial. A judge who is ready to make allowances for an error or two can really 'lose faith' in a claimant who they feel has wrongly certified a document as true, just as they can where a person has badly exaggerated a disability.

MEDICAL EVIDENCE WHICH MUST BE SERVED WITH THE PARTICULARS OF CLAIM

316. The Particulars of Claim must be served with medical evidence which relates your injuries to the accident. In the most simple case, where the injuries were modest and recovered quickly, this may be a report by a GP. At the other end of the spectrum, there may be a number of reports from experts in a range of different specialisms, dealing with devastating life long injuries and needs.

A VITAL POINT TO KEEP IN MIND: VOLUNTEER IMPROVEMENTS IN YOUR CAPABILITIES

317. While dealing with 'credibility' and the statement of truth, it is also worth explaining that it is very important to tell the medical experts, your solicitor and others if your condition improves significantly, and/or if you need less help, or you can undertake a chore/task which had previously required assistance.

318. By doing so, you are demonstrating that you are a truthful person, which is extremely important. You should make sure your solicitor communicates such improvement to the insurer, because as well as potentially making your claim smaller (a reasonable consequence of your improvement) it will inform the insurer (and later the judge) that you are someone to be trusted and relied on when you give evidence on all of the other issues in your claim. That will give you an excellent platform to achieve a good settlement of the claim.

319. It is also very valuable if and when the defendant serves surveillance evidence, because you can demonstrate that any apparent improvements in your condition were already reported to your solicitor, before you became aware of the surveillance.

SECTION 18: FURTHER STAGES IN THE LITIGATION

320. I have provided a short summary of the most typical stages in a case at the end of the guide. The following 'timetable' is an illustration only, as each case will have its own timetable tailored to the issues.

THE DEFENDANT'S DOCUMENTS IN RESPONSE

321. The defendant must respond to your litigation documents by serving a 'Defence' and a 'Counter-Schedule', which in general terms, set out its position in relation to the allegations, and losses you have claimed. These documents also require a statement of truth.

ALLOCATION TO A 'TRACK'

322. There are a number of stages after the service of the Defence. The first is the 'allocation' of the claim into a 'track'. This takes place on the first occasion that the Court deals with the claim. The judge decides (with suggestions from the parties) into which 'track' the claim should be placed (or 'allocated').

323. There are three tracks. The first is 'small claims track', which is broadly used for disputes which involve smaller sums of money. Injury claims where the injury itself commands compensation of under £1,000 are usually dealt with in the small claims track. Remember that road traffic claims valued up to £10,000 must be dealt with through a government scheme known as 'the 'Portal' (**see the link on the website**).

324. Next are 'fast track claims', which are expected to have a value of £25,000 or less. Last, there are 'multi-track claims', which are expected to have a value exceeding £25,000.

A TYPICAL SMALL CLAIM

325. A very high proportion of injury claims concern a relatively short-lived injury, such as a fractured bone, or a modest whiplash injury. These often have a very painful (or 'acute') initial phase, followed by a recovery phase, sometimes over a period of weeks or months. In a case where the initial

injury recovers completely within a few weeks, and there may be a week or two off work, and some additional expenses (travel to hospital, medicine, etc.) the claim is almost certainly a 'small claim'.

A TYPICAL FAST TRACK CLAIM

326. Where the injury is more serious and/or may not fully recover (take considerably longer to recover), and the earnings loss is greater (perhaps a month or more), and the individual required considerable initial family assistance, and incurred heavier costs and expenses (e.g. physiotherapy costs), the claim is very likely to be allocated to the fast track.

A TYPICAL MULTI-TRACK CLAIM

327. In almost all cases in which the injured person continues to suffer significant symptoms and/or restrictions as a result of the accident, particularly where these have lead to a long term reduction in his ability to work, and ongoing claims for assistance with tasks that they would otherwise have managed, the claim is likely to be allocated to the multi track. The same is of course true for very serious cases, in which a person suffers life changing injuries (e.g. brain injuries, incompletely recovered multiple injuries, amputations, and cases involving permanent significant pain).

328. There are some potentially important consequences of allocation. One is that (in a nutshell), the Court tends to be less flexible about allowing parties to rely upon experts in different disciplines in fast track claims. However, the significance of these issues are best explained (as and when relevant) by your representatives.

SEEKING CLARIFICATION OF THE OTHER SIDE'S CASE

329. The parties may seek clarification of each other's case, or can ask the other side to admit certain facts, so that they are no longer in dispute. This can be a useful tactical opportunity to 'smoke out' the other party, i.e. force them to reveal a weakness in their case.

OBTAINING FURTHER EXPERT EVIDENCE – (I) MEDICAL

330. Once the claim has been started the Court will make decisions, called 'directions' (set out in 'Court Orders') which 'direct' the parties how the case will progress. Included in these are directions concerning the expert evidence which the parties may rely upon in presenting the claim.

331. In a simple case, the initial GP report may be sufficient to explain the injuries and their consequences, and the defendant may accept its contents. In that case, the parties will try to negotiate a settlement on the basis of that medical evidence.

332. In a more serious case, with longer lasting physical injuries (perhaps following a fracture, or a soft tissue injury to the back or neck), the evidence is likely to be provided by a more specialist expert, the most familiar of which is an orthopaedic surgeon. In general terms, a different expert is required to assist the Court with specialist evidence for each (significant) separate injury.

'JOINTLY' AND 'SOLELY' INSTRUCTED EXPERTS

333. Where the injuries of a particular type are unlikely to be controversial, or may not contribute a great deal to the overall claim, the court may order a report to be provided by a 'single joint expert' (or 'joint expert') in a 'joint report'. The critical difference between a jointly instructed expert, and an expert instructed by one party alone, is that a joint expert cannot discuss the case in private with either side. An expert instructed by one party alone (a 'sole instruction') is permitted to discuss the claim with that side's lawyers and the client, to consider all of the issues relating to his expertise, and comment on the opinion of the other side's expert. In larger cases, and most multi-track cases, the court usually permits each party to instruct the most important experts on a sole basis.

334. The joint expert is instructed by both parties together. He provides a report, and may, if necessary, then be asked questions to clarify his opinion. In most cases, that evidence will be considered in writing by the court, if the claim does not settle. However, in some cases, the expert may be required to attend the trial.

335. Also, more importantly, if one of the parties considers that the report is unsatisfactory (perhaps because of its reasoning, the conclusion, or for other reasons) the unhappy party can request the court's permission to rely upon the opinion of another expert in the same field.

336. The rules specifically require the court to limit expert evidence to that which is "reasonably required to determine the proceedings" (i.e. to resolve the issues in dispute). Therefore, any party seeking to replace a joint expert (or indeed its own expert – see **section 13**) should provide careful and persuasive reasons to the court.

OBTAINING FURTHER EXPERT EVIDENCE – (II) NON-MEDICAL

337. There is also an opportunity, if it is reasonably required, for the parties to obtain non-medical expert evidence in disciplines relevant to the claims you have made. These might involve the following experts:

(a) An expert on the liability issues, which might be road traffic reconstruction, or commenting on the safety of a workplace;

(b) A forensic accountant, who can assist in analysing the financial consequences of the accident (often to a person's business, or income);

(c) An employment expert, who should assist the Court with specific evidence about your career prospects (i) if the accident had not happened, and (ii) now that it has happened;

(d) An occupational therapist, if you have serious physical restrictions, to assess your ongoing domestic needs.

DISCLOSURE

338. There will come a time when your solicitor asks you to assist with 'disclosure'. This is a relatively straightforward process for the exchange of documents relevant to the case. Where liability is in dispute, an employer's documents (e.g. concerning working practices, training, risk assessment) are likely to be crucial. As far as you are concerned, the process typically relates to documents concerning:

(a) your losses (such as pre- and post-accident payslips, any/all receipts for money spent, etc.);

(b) any state benefits you are receiving. These will include disability living allowance, incapacity benefit, etc., as well as some locally assessed benefits (for example where a local authority has assessed your need for domestic support). Typically, this documentation includes benefit applications and assessments – it is just as important that you have provided accurate information in applying for these benefits as you do within the claim.

SHORT COURT HEARINGS AND APPLICATIONS

339. During the claim, there are often short hearings (for example a 'case management conference') in which the Court takes stock of the issues in the case and makes 'directions' about the future steps needed to guide the claim towards a trial date (something which also focuses the parties on the need to continue to prepare their case, and to try to settle the claim before the trial).

340. Also, there is an opportunity for the parties to make 'applications' during the claim. Applications are typically requests for permission to do something, or requests that the Court orders the other party to do something. These often include requests:

(a) for information or documentation the other party is declining to provide;

(b) for permission to rely upon an expert witness in a new discipline;

(c) for an interim payment (**section 19**).

JOINT REPORTS OF THE EXPERT WITNESSES

341. At some point, usually towards the end of the timetable, the Court will have ordered that the expert witnesses on either side should have a discussion and produce a joint report. This is a potentially critical document. It reflects the only occasion when the expert witnesses discuss their opinion. During the discussion, they are intended to identify the points upon which they agree, and the points on which they disagree. They are then required to set out those matters in a written report, in which they also provide their reasons for the remaining disagreements.

342. At this point it is probably sensible to refresh your memory on the points in **section 13**.

EXCHANGE OF WITNESS STATEMENTS AND FINAL SCHEDULES

343. Generally the final stage of the process is the 'exchange' of witness statements, and a final 'Schedule of Loss' and 'Counter-Schedule'. At that point the parties will have a very clear idea of the claims being advanced, and the arguments against those claims, as well as all of the evidence each party intends to rely upon to establish its arguments.

SECTION 19: INTERIM PAYMENTS

344. One of the worst predicaments for an injured person is that they cease to be able to bring home a wage. They may also incur considerable expenditure, perhaps in treatment, medication, travel costs and the like. The absence of income can very quickly spiral into debt. Debt is debilitating, humiliating and depressing. It will make dealing with an adversarial process even more daunting.

345. An 'interim payment' is the legal name for a payment 'on account' of your claim.

CASES IN WHICH LIABILITY IS ADMITTED OR SETTLED

346. In virtually all cases in which 'liability' is agreed by the insurer, or where the proportions of blame between the parties can be agreed by negotiation, your representatives should seek an interim payment. There are strict rules about such applications, but they are not difficult to satisfy providing liability has been resolved. Some solicitors need prompting to ask the insurer for an interim payment, because some of their clients prefer to have all of the damages at the end of the claim. However, that is often because few claimants appreciate how much longer the claim may take to resolve.

347. It is important to make it clear to your solicitor that you will need funds as soon as possible.

348. It is also important to understand that if the defendant refuses to make an 'interim' payment, the only way to obtain one is by making an application to the Court. It is obvious that your solicitors can only ask the Court for an interim payment if the claim has been commenced at Court.

349. There are occasionally situations in which it may be tactically preferable not to issue the claim until close to the three years deadline. However, you are entitled to be given a good reason by your solicitor why this is the case. It seems that some solicitors have got into the habit of waiting until near the deadline to issue all of their claims. That is very unlikely to benefit all of their clients.

350. Once the claim has started, you can 'apply' (i.e. ask the Court) to order the defendant to make an interim payment. You are entitled to receive a sum which is 'not more than a reasonable proportion of your likely final award'. The Court usually judges the sum quite conservatively because if it awards you a sum larger than you are awarded at the trial, the defendant will have to recover the 'overpayment' from you after the claim ends.

351. Still, in most cases, it is easy to obtain an interim payment, and it can make the injured person's life considerably more comfortable and less difficult.

CASES IN WHICH LIABILITY IS WHOLLY DISPUTED

352. It is much more difficult to obtain an interim payment in a case in which the defendant disputes liability. That is because you are unlikely to persuade the Court of the relevant legal test, which is that, at a trial, you "would be likely to recover substantial damages."

CASES IN WHICH LIABILITY IS PARTIALLY DISPUTED

353. These are cases, discussed in **section 3**, in which there is a risk of losing a proportion of the damages because of contributory fault. It is usually still possible to achieve an interim payment, because you should be able to prove that you will obtain judgment for a proportion of your claim. However, in order that you are not awarded more than your claim may be worth the 'not more than a reasonable proportion' figure, will also have to take into account the range of possible outcomes for your contributory fault.

WHEN AND HOW CLAIMS END

—
PART FIVE
—

SECTION 20: WHEN IS IT TIME TO SETTLE MY CLAIM?

354. In general terms, perhaps the most important consideration is that you receive a settled medical prognosis and a settled employment 'prognosis' before the claim concludes. That is because once the case is finished (whether by settlement or trial) then, except in very rare cases, it cannot be re-opened.

355. A settled medical prognosis cannot always be achieved, perhaps because some further treatment is necessary. The same is true of employment, where a job search (or re-training) may not have started, let alone have finished.

356. Also, the defendant may have made a 'generous' offer (in terms of the available evidence) in order to achieve an early settlement before your evidence is complete, to try to avoid paying escalating costs, which may create tension and pressure on the claimant's side: **section 22 - 23**.

357. Claims rarely settle at the perfect time, but as long as you are aware of what you need in order to settle (i.e. a measure of certainty on the important issues) you can usually achieve a fair settlement at an appropriate time.

THE FINAL COURT DOCUMENTS

358. After the completion of the medical evidence, disclosure, exchange of statements, and final Schedule of Loss and Counter-Schedule the parties usually turn their attention to trying to achieve the certainty of a settlement, rather than both sides taking the risk of having a trial which could end up with one of them achieving a much worse result than they could negotiate.

SECTION 21: OFFERS TO SETTLE

359. The whole purpose of 'offers' is to promote settlement, essentially by creating pressure on the other side.

360. The Court rules allow parties to make any number of offers to each other (on 'liability', contributory negligence, and quantum) before and during the claim process.

361. That pressure is created for a claimant because if a 'reasonable' offer is made (and not accepted) early on, or at least before some substantial part of the costs are incurred, the claimant's side is likely to have to pay all of the subsequent costs if the claim later settles for less, or if, at trial, the judge awards less.

362. The pressure is created for a defendant because if a claimant has made a 'reasonable' offer and the claim later concludes for a higher sum, the rules provide for the defendant to pay considerable additional interest on the claimant's compensation and costs, from shortly after the offer was made.

363. There are many different ways to use offers to create pressure (e.g. making offers to settle parts of a claim). Consequently, the use of offers can create significant tension on both sides, as well as achieving good results and avoiding trials.

AN EXAMPLE OF TENSION CREATED BY A DEFENDANT OFFER

364. A claimant may have been hoping to recover £100,000. His lawyers have said that, at trial, the judge is most likely to award £80,000 - £110,000. The wide £30,000 bracket may be because an important part of the claim depends on the judge accepting that the claimant would probably have received a work promotion after the accident.

365. The defendant then skilfully makes an offer of £80,000. What happens next?
    (a) The claimant's lawyers will have to advise the BTE or ATE insurer whether the offer is 'reasonable';
    (b) Even if the lawyer gives the range of possible award, it is likely that the

insurer will not want to provide continued insurance cover, because if the claimant was awarded £80,000 at trial, the BTE/ATE insurer would have to pay all of the defendant's costs from 21 days after the offer was made;

(c) That means that unless the 'team' (client, solicitor and barrister) can provide good reasons to persuade the insurer to 'stay on board' unless a higher offer is made, the claimant could be left high and dry - knowing the offer is within, but at the bottom of, his representatives' range, but is left with the horrid choice of accepting it, or continuing the claim with no further 'cover' from his own insurer.

(d) If that did happen, his solicitor will also have to tell the defendant that the insurance cover has been withdrawn, effectively telling the defendant that they consider that the offer was acceptable.

366. That situation illustrates how vital it is:

(a) To have a trusting relationship with your representatives;

(b) That your representatives construct your claim with professionalism and precision from the earliest possible stage – so that you have the best possible idea of the range of value of the claim before offers are made.

A SECOND TYPE OF DIFFICULT OFFER

367. Some insurers may decide very early on (for several reasons) that a case would be far better settled sooner than later. They might even make a very rough calculation, erring towards a 'generous' assessment of several potential claims, in order to make a 'telling' early offer, which exerts pressure on the claimant's side.

368. It can be very stressful and disorientating to receive an offer of that type very early on, because you may be nowhere near a settled medical state, and/or may not be in a position to assess the long term impact of your injuries.

369. What will happen if your condition improved so much that a claim thought to be worth £100,000 turns out to be worth £50,000, when the defendant offered to settle the claim a year or more earlier for the same sum? It is difficult to predict the outcome in every case (i.e. whether the claimant's side will have to pay the defendant's costs from shortly after the offer),

and it is important to 'take stock' of the claim in light of such an offer, perhaps in a conference with the solicitor and barrister, and referring to all the medical evidence which is available (e.g. notes and correspondence from your treating doctors).

370. It may simply be impossible to assess the value of the claim, in which case your solicitor should thank the defendant for the offer but explain, in as much detail as possible, why the offer cannot be considered at that point in time. Provided there are good reasons why the offer cannot be considered, then there is a good prospect that your representatives can prevent the usual costs consequences of not accepting what turns out later to have been a good offer.

371. Also, in such a situation, the insurer which is indemnifying ('covering') you against exposure to a costs order in favour of the Defendant is unlikely to withdraw their 'cover'.

"FIRST OFFER SYNDROME"

372. There are some cases in which a party makes a low initial offer, then a higher offer, for example as the medical evidence becomes clearer and reveals a worse prognosis for the claimant. Equally, there are cases in which a larger initial offer is withdrawn (and replaced by a lower offer) when the case changes, for example if the prognosis improves, or when a defendant considers that the claimant has lost credibility, perhaps after there has been a report from a defendant-instructed expert, or some surveillance which could impair the claimant's credibility.

373. There are some (increasingly rare) insurers who make low "first" offers simply to set the scene for a better offer/s. Some claimants suggest (usually citing the experience of a friend) that no first offer should ever be accepted, because "there is always more money in the pot." That is the wrong approach – and should not be confused with tactics during settlement negotiations (see **section 24**). Do not forget that a key reason for a defendant to make an offer is to provide itself with protection against paying costs to your side.

374. When you receive any offer, you should assess it on its merits. The offer should be rejected if there are good reasons why your side concludes that it will be beaten by a reasonable margin.

SECTION 22: WHAT IF SOMETHING GOES WRONG AND/OR I FEEL PRESSURED TO SETTLE?

PRESSURE TO SETTLE FROM YOUR 'OWN SIDE'

375. It is particularly important not to be pressurised into settling your claim. There may be sensible reasons why a claim should be settled. If so, the reasons should be clearly and carefully explained to you, and put into writing at your request.

376. If the reasons have not been explained, or you do not understand and/or agree with them, you should seek a second opinion.

377. If the advice has come from the solicitor, you should ask for a conference with a barrister. If it has come from the solicitor and a barrister (and you still feel unhappy), you should ask your solicitor for a conference with a second barrister. There may be costs implications of being provided with further advice, but if there is a lot at stake (in terms of the overall claim) it will be worthwhile to obtain a second opinion even if the costs may not be recoverable from the defendant. As regards replacing your representatives, see **section 6 - 7**.

378. The reason it is so important to be satisfied about the reason for settling a claim is because it is much better to conclude your claim against the original defendant at a reasonable level, than have to make another claim, later on, against your original representatives.

WHY A SECOND CLAIM IS WORSE THAN CHANGING LAWYERS IN THE FIRST CLAIM

379. First and foremost, you will have had enough of litigation!

380. Also, a second claim is an entirely different legal animal from the first claim. In the first, you are suing someone for the damage caused by their fault. In the second, whilst you are suing for the damage caused by the fault of your representative/s, that is actually a claim for the chance of what you did not achieve in the first claim.

381. To get the second claim off the ground, you have to prove (and here we have to return to 'causation' - **section 14**) that your representatives were negligent in handling your claim, which can be very difficult as many failures and errors fall short of 'negligence' and that the specific negligence you can prove actually caused your loss.

382. Last, but not least, it is likely to be difficult for you to obtain funding for a second claim unless it is very clear cut.

383. If, however, something does go very badly wrong in your claim, it is possible that you may have to consider bringing a claim against your own representatives. Happily, for everyone's sake, this is rare.

SECTION 23: A CONFERENCE AFTER THE EVIDENCE IS COMPLETE

384. You may have a very clear idea of the parameters of your claim, either from written advice from the solicitor or barrister, or from a previous conference. However, very often, by the time witness statements and Schedule/Counter-Schedule have been exchanged, the goalposts may have shifted both in terms of risks and valuation (in relation to some or all issues in the case).

385. If that is the case, there is no harm in requesting an updating conference with your solicitor and barrister and, perhaps, a written estimate (even on a single sheet of paper) setting out for each loss in dispute: the figures in the Schedule, those in the Counter-Schedule, and perhaps a 'reasonable' column, which sets out what you can expect to be awarded by the judge at trial. Of course, many barristers will have different ways of advising you, and expressing risk, so do not be too rigid in what you expect. You do, however, need specific, reasoned advice.

386. A short written summary often does assist you to consider written offers, and offers at any settlement meeting, and it will make it easier to discuss the level of award for each of the claims.

SECTION 24: JOINT SETTLEMENT MEETINGS

387. Many claims, particularly larger claims, now settle at a joint settlement meeting ('JSM'), which typically takes place after the evidence is finalised, Schedule of Loss and Counter-Schedule served, but some time before the trial. The timing usually enables the parties, after a failed JSM, to make offers which will still have some significant costs consequences for the other party after the trial.

388. Generally a JSM involves discussions between the opposing barristers, with their respective teams (claimant and solicitor: insurer and solicitor) in nearby rooms. Both sides have an opportunity to explain their position to each other on a 'without prejudice' basis (i.e. in a way which will never be revealed to the judge), and to try to persuade each other that they are correct.

389. JSM's have the benefit to the claimant of enabling him to participate in the attempt at settlement, considering arguments from the defendant, and not having to experience the stress and risk of a trial.

390. It is also worth noting that it is rare for a claimant to meet the opposing side before or during the JSM, and he would never be forced to do so. After a settlement at a JSM, both parties very often shake hands and wish each other well.

391. JSMs have the benefit for the insurer of allowing them to make their best offer of settlement before running the risk of paying (very high) trial costs.

392. Unlike written offers (**see section 21**), it is very unusual to accept a 'first offer' at a JSM. Where the parties both consider it worthwhile to have a JSM, there is (generally) an exchange of offers before 'final offers' are made.

393. In a rare case, a party might only make one offer, or reiterate an old offer, because it feels very strong in that position (and will very probably give detailed reasons at the JSM). But, in general, negotiations at a JSM will continue until one side specifically states that it is making its 'final offer'. Those are the magic words, which communicate that that is as far as that party will go at the JSM.

394. It is worth noting that defendants often follow up a failed JSM with a slightly lower offer, which they then defend at the trial. In other words, and understandably, the insurer usually makes their best offer to settle at the JSM.

395. In a nutshell, then, the JSM provides the parties with the benefit of achieving a certain result without involving the court.

SECTION 25: MEDIATION/ALTERNATIVE DISPUTE RESOLUTION

396. In order to maximise the prospects of concluding cases without involving the Court, a process of mediation (or 'ADR') has grown up in recent years. It is still in its infancy in the personal injury field, but it is bound to increase with time.

397. The idea of ADR is that a "mediator", independent of both parties, attempts to 'bring them together' to reach a settlement. In general terms, the mediator 'facilitates' a settlement by listening to the respective parties, and communicating with both of them. The mediator is really a highly trained and experienced 'go-between', but many of them are skilled and do manage to bring parties together to settlement.

398. There are certain situations in which the parties may decide to meet at a JSM, and others in which mediation may be preferred. Each case will depend on the precise circumstances.

SECTION 26: TRIAL

399. It is extremely unlikely that you will have to 'go to Court' (in other words have a 'trial'). There are rare cases in which it is unavoidable that disputes between parties require determination by a judge, but more trials probably take place because of an avoidable breakdown in the relationship between the parties.

400. Providing your claim has been put together carefully and reasonably, there is no need to be frightened into settling your claim below a reasonable level by the prospect of a trial.

401. If the parties remain at loggerheads on 'liability', 'contributory negligence', and/or on part, or all, of the 'valuation' issues, both may make their final offers then proceed to trial. Both sides will by this time know that the successful side is very likely to recover the costs of the trial, which represent the bulk of the costs of the claim.

402. It is also quite possible that one side, or even both, feel sufficiently confident that they will not increase an older offer. That reflects the fact that, in broad terms, the older the offer that a party 'betters' at trial, the more beneficial the costs consequences for that party.

403. If a case does end in a trial, it is more important than ever that the injured person understands the process and trusts those representing him. The thought of a 'trial' can be daunting, and needs careful explanation.

404. The trial will involve a judge (not a jury), factual witnesses (including you), expert witnesses (depending on the issues in dispute), and the respective lawyers. Trials take place in 'public', in that anyone may attend, but it is very rare indeed for anyone unconnected to the case to 'watch' a trial.

405. The procedure at trial is that the claimant presents his case, with factual and expert evidence (**see section 12**), followed by the defendant presenting its case. Each factual witness is required to promise to tell the truth. This entails 'taking an oath', which involves stating that your evidence will be truthful. Witnesses who have a religious belief take the oath while holding a relevant religious book (such as the bible).

406. Do remember that the two key reasons so few cases reach a trial are because (i) trials are extremely expensive, and (ii) the outcome is always uncertain.

407. Of course, one side may have made an obvious error of judgment in deciding to 'fight' the case, but generally when both parties decide to contest a trial, their decision reflects confidence in their own position. Therefore, in almost every case which 'goes to trial', both parties have taken that decision because they believe a trial will provide a better result than the best settlement terms on offer.

GIVING EVIDENCE AT A TRIAL

408. It is worth bearing in mind that trials are inevitably stressful. The 'countdown' to such an important day may be difficult to cope with, and can make people anxious. The claimant may well be worried that he will look very nervous, perhaps because he may never have spoken in public before, let alone being carefully questioned about events some years earlier.

409. In fact, there is nothing to worry about - the judge has a great deal of experience and will expect a person unfamiliar with the system to be nervous.

410. All you have to do at a trial, in actual fact, is listen carefully to questions, and answer truthfully. If you cannot remember something, that is the truthful answer.

411. It is always better to admit, truthfully, to having forgotten something than to grasp at a fading recollection and try to perfect it. Similarly, it is always a mistake to try to rationalise events, or re-create a recollection during questioning.

FINAL WORD ABOUT TRIALS

412. When both parties ask a third party (the judge) to determine a range of issues, that introduces a wide range of possible outcomes, from your 'best case' to the defendant's 'best case', so that you need, as a team, to be confident in your position/s before proceeding to trial.

SECTION 27: APPEAL

413. In a short case, lasting a day or less, the judge will often 'deliver judgment' at the end of the day, or the next morning. This will involve setting out the issues in dispute, the evidence deployed by the parties on those issues, deciding which party was correct, and giving reasons for the decision. In longer cases, or where there is significant reading involved, the judge may well need time to reflect on the evidence, and legal arguments, so that there is a delay before the judgment is 'handed down' (often in typed form).

414. After the parties have had an opportunity to digest the judgment, the losing party (or even a party who won some issues but lost on a substantial issue) may consider whether to challenge the judge's decision and reasoning. This process is called an appeal, and it is only generally available when the judge has made a clear error in his reasoning, or in applying the law.

THE AWARD AND EFFECT OF COMPENSATION

—
PART SIX
—

SECTION 28: LUMP SUM OR PERIODICAL SUM

415. In the vast majority of cases the award of damages is paid as a single 'lump sum', comprising all of the claims agreed between the parties, or ordered at trial. In larger cases, where there are ongoing losses and restrictions (typically lost earnings and care requirements) parts of the award can be made payable at regular intervals. These are known as Periodical Payments (or 'PP'). A crucial benefit of a PP is that it can be designed to keep pace with the cost of the loss which it is compensating.

416. In past years, the increase in costs of purchasing 'care' has been higher than increases in the general cost of living. If that trend continues, a severely injured person whose compensation is calculated now, at today's costs, would in fact run out of money in the future, because it would cost him more money as the years passed to buy the same level of care.

417. With a PP, the payments will continue for as long as the defendant's responsibility for the loss continues. In a typical case, of a substantial continuing care need for life, where a person has suffered a severe brain injury, the PP will come to an end when the Claimant dies.

418. Another benefit is that the level of PP can be adjusted to take account of likely variations in the person's needs.

419. Lastly, having a PP in a claim which will last for the claimant's lifetime eliminates the need to explore how long the claimant is likely to live. A person's 'life expectancy', as it is known, may or may not have been significantly affected by the accident injuries.

420. Trying to calculate a lump sum award requires the multiplication of an annual cost by a figure to reflect the claimant's likely life expectancy. There may well be a wide range of opinions on life expectancy, making it very distressing and difficult to deal with such issues.

421. In those circumstances, having a PP for life can be very attractive. It protects the claimant for the whole of his life, and it ensures that the defendant will only have to pay compensation while the claimant is alive.

422. As you can imagine, PP's raise interesting and complicated issues which you will need to discuss with your representatives.

423. In some cases, the parties settle on a 'lump sum' which is intended to provide the injured person with compensation for a long period, possibly until their death. If the award is not made on a PP basis (for which there may be good reasons), you will need to seek out immediate, skilled financial advice, to guide you to make the best quality decisions possible when investing your award. Your solicitor should be able to direct you towards an appropriate independent advisor.

SECTION 29: PRESERVING YOUR BENEFITS AFTER THE CLAIM HAS FINISHED

424. Often state benefits may be a lifeline to an injured person whose claim has been protracted, particularly if no interim payment has been available.

425. For a host of reasons, at the end of the claim, the injured person may be very keen not to lose his entitlement to state benefits (not least, if the claim has recovered much less compensation than was hoped). Many benefit applications require the application to provide details of their capital assets and/or income, and to update that information if the situation changes. It is frequently the case that the amount of a person's compensation would disqualify him from receiving certain benefits. However, the law provides a simple legal mechanism by which the injured party can, in appropriate circumstances, receive compensation without losing state benefits. This is by setting up a 'Personal Injury Trust'.

426. Any firm of solicitors who advises you on your claim should be able to refer you to an advisor who can assist you to set up a 'PI Trust'. It is sensible to set this process in motion early on, ideally before you receive an interim payment.

SECTION 30: PROVISIONAL COMPENSATION – A RARE EXCEPTION TO FINALITY IN CLAIMS

427. There is one, very rare, example in which the award of compensation is provisional rather than final (whether by lump sum or PP).

428. Provisional compensation may be awarded by the Court if there is a risk that a person's injury could lead, at some point in the future, to a significant deterioration in their health (and consequently to their needs).

429. It is generally only relevant in situations in which the injured person has a very small risk of something very serious happening (such as developing epilepsy, or becoming blind), which could substantially change their life.

430. In such a case, the Court may (but does not have to) award damages on the basis that the condition does not occur, and to permit the person to apply to the Court if the small risk is, in fact, realised.

FINAL THOUGHTS

—
PART SEVEN
—

SECTION 31: FINAL THOUGHTS

431. This guide is intended to assist you to resolve you claim by ensuring that you understand the nature and structure of the process.

432. My final thoughts are:

    (a) If something matters to you, mention it to those representing you;

    (b) Make sure you get answers to questions you raise, with reasons for those answers. If you do not, you will need to consider whether you are being well represented;

    (c) Do not stick your head in the sand if something happens which is detrimental to your claim, or if you are worried about facing up to an error or inconsistency in the evidence;

    (d) Remember that being untruthful or inaccurate is likely to harm your claim significantly, and assume that untruths, errors or inaccuracies will be discovered.

433. It is hoped that as a consequence of following the advice in this guide, you will be able to take your claim forward, with confidence, knowing that you have a very good chance of reaching a fair and reasonable settlement.

ADDITIONAL MATERIALS

PART EIGHT

EXPLANATION OF TERMS IN THE GUIDE

ADR
alternative dispute resolution (**section 25**)

Adversarial system
the nature of the English legal system which makes claimants and defendants 'adversaries' to reach a fair result (**section 1**)

Advocacy
presenting a case in Court (**section 4**)

Amenity
loss of enjoyment (**section 3**)

Application
request to the Court (**section 18**)

ATE
'after the event' insurance (**section 8**)

BTE
'before the event' insurance (**section 8**)

Burden of proof
which party must prove a particular issue (**section 14**)

'But for'
'in the absence of', usually in the context of what would have happened in a person's life 'but for' the accident (**section 14**)

'Causation'
the reason why something happened (**section 14**)

CFA
conditional fee agreement – 'no win-no fee' (**section 8**)

Chambers
a barrister's office

Claim Form
The formal Court document which commences court proceedings (**section 17**)

CICA
Criminal Injuries Compensation Authority (**section 9**)

CMC
case management conference, a short hearing in which to take stock of issues, and may deal with 'applications' (**section 18**)

Conference/'con'
a meeting with your solicitor and barrister

CPR
Civil Procedure Rules – the rules governing the procedure of claims

Cross examination
being asked questions by the defendant's barrister during a trial (**section 26**)

CRU
Compensation Recovery Unit – a government body within the DWP, which provides a definitive certificate of the benefits you have received since the accident

Directions
see 'Orders', below

Disbursements
sums of money spent (for e.g. on expert's reports) during the claim

Disclosure
The process of revealing relevant documents to another party (**section 18**)

DWP
Department of Work and Pensions – who provide benefits information in the form of CRU certificates

Examination in chief
being asked questions by your barrister during a trial (**section 26**)

Expert
a witness who provides evidence of opinion not fact (**section 12**)

Fault
the basis of 'liability' (similar to 'responsibility'/'blame')

Filing
sending a document to the court

Firm
a solicitor's organisation (**section 4**)

Hearing
a meeting between the parties and a judge, including a CMC, application, or trial

HSE
Health and Safety Executive (**section 15**)

Instructions
the formal term for a request by a solicitor to a barrister to provide work (**section 4**). Also used to describe the letter provided to expert witnesses when seeking an opinion

Interim payment
money provided to a claimant 'on account' (**section 19**)

Joint expert
(also single joint expert) an expert who receives his instructions from both parties. This is usually seen in a small or moderate case, where the evidence is unlikely to be controversial, or in a more serious case, where the injury covered by this expert is likely to be a substantial part of the overall claim

Joint report
A report prepared by opposing expert witnesses in the same field which sets out all of the areas in the case within their expertise, on which they agree, and disagree, and giving reasons for disagreement (**section 18**)

JSM
joint settlement meeting (**section 24**)

Liability
see fault, above

Limitation period
time permitted in which to make a claim (usually three years from the accident)

Mediation
a process aimed at settling a claim which is assisted by an independent person (**section 25**)

MIB
Motor Insurer's Bureau (**section 9**)

Mitigation of loss
taking reasonable steps to limit the consequences of an injury (**section 3**)

Oath
a solemn promise to tell the truth (**section 26**)

Orders
judicial decisions (an example is a 'directions order', which sets out certain steps required of the parties within a specified period)

Particulars of Claim
the formal document setting out your claim (**section 17**)

Party/Parties
an individual or organisation involved in a claim

PI Trust
Personal Injury Trust – a method of investing compensation to protect your benefits (**section 29**)

PPO
Periodical Payments Order – a manner of being paid compensation on a regular basis instead of in one lump sum – particularly relevant in cases with a great deal of future earnings loss or care (**section 28**)

PSLA
Pain, suffering and loss of amenity (**section 3**)

Quantum
a word for the value of a claim

Redacted
erasing parts of a document (**section 13**)

Re-examination
being asked question by your barrister after cross examination (see above)

Regulations
legal rules made under the authority of a statute (see below)

RIDDOR
A Health and Safety (HSE, see above) document short for "Report of injury, disease or dangerous occurrence" (**Section 15**)

RTA
road traffic accident

Schedule of Loss
a document setting out financial claims (**section 17**)

Served
sending a document to another party

Special damages
financial losses from the accident to trial or settlement (**section 3/16**)

Split trial
a trial on one issue (usually 'liability', or 'fault') only (**section 12**)

Standard of proof
the level of proof needed (**section 14**)

Statement of truth
certification at the end of a document that the facts in the document are true (**section 17**)

Statute
an Act of Parliament (and see Regulations, above)

'Without prejudice'/'WP'
a private discussion between parties (usually negotiations during settlement discussions)

PART 8

STAGES IN A TYPICAL INJURY CLAIM

1.	Meeting/discussion between injured person and solicitor:	**section 15**
2.	Solicitor instructed (terms of business agreed):	**section 4**
3.	Letter of claim sent to defendant:	**section 17**
4.	Response to letter of claim (disclosure if liability disputed):	**section 18**
5.	Claimant obtains medical evidence:	**section 12**
6.	Claimant requests interim payment:	**section 19**
7.	Defendant obtains medical evidence:	**section 18**
8.	Attempts made to settle claim before proceedings issued	
9.	Claim Form issued:	**section 17**
10.	Claim Form, Particulars, Schedule, medical evidence served:	**section 17**
11.	Service of Defence, Counter-Schedule:	**section 18**
12.	Allocation of claim to a track:	**section 18**
13.	Questions posed to opposing party to clarify issues in dispute:	**section 18**
14.	Questions posed to respective experts to clarify issues:	**section 18**
15.	Formal disclosure of relevant documentation:	**section 18**
16.	Witness statements exchanged:	**section 18**
17.	Service of further medical/non-medical expert evidence:	**section 18**
18.	Joint statements by medical and non/medical expert witness:	**section 18**
19.	Final Schedule of Loss served:	**section 20**
20.	Final Counter-Schedule served:	**section 20**
21.	Joint settlement meeting often takes place (or 'mediation'):	**section 25**
22.	Trial:	**section 26**

QUESTIONS FOR YOUR SOLICITOR – OR REPLACEMENT SOLICITOR

1. What are your qualifications and experience?

2. Can you give me an example of a similar claim that you have dealt with?

3. Will you personally handle my claim? If not, what are the qualifications of the person who will, and can I meet him before deciding how to proceed?

4. How will my claim be funded?

5. Who will fund all necessary medical reports and other 'disbursements' incurred during the claim?

6. Will I be exposed to any risk of paying money to anyone involved in my case, and if so, in what circumstances, and why?

7. Will the firm make any deductions from any interim payments that the defendant agrees, or that are ordered by the Court?

8. Will your firm receive a commission or any other financial advantage from anyone involved in the claim?

9. At what stage might you involve a barrister in my claim?

10. Is there any restriction on the barrister/s who can be instructed?

11. Will you obtain and personally review my medical records before instructing medical experts?

12. Will you collate my medical records into paginated sections and let me have a copy myself if I want one?

13. Do you instruct medical experts direct or do you rely upon a medical agency and in either case how do you ensure the quality and relevant expertise of the expert?

14. Will you carefully review any medical evidence (in light of the medical notes, and my evidence) before serving it?

15. How, and how frequently, will you update me on the progress of my claim?

16. At the end of the claim, will I receive all of the damages agreed with the defendant (or ordered by the Court) or could my compensation be reduced in any way?

CLIENT CHECKLISTS ON LIABILITY AND VALUATION ISSUES (FROM SECTION 16)

LIABILITY / THE FAULT ISSUE

1. Write down an account of the accident as soon as you can.

2. Take several photos immediately after any accident, to illustrate what happened, the position of vehicles, a piece of dangerous equipment, etc.

3. Consider who else might be able to provide information about the accident.

4. Consider who else could provide evidence in a broader context (e.g. in a workplace claim) on issues relating to training, or equipment.

5. In a workplace claim, note down names and addresses of colleagues who leave the defendant's employment who might provide evidence concerning liability issues, or valuation issues (e.g. your reputation, opportunities for promotion, etc.).

VALUATION / LOSS OF EARNINGS OR INCOME

1. Keep anything which will help to show how you have earned your living both before and after the accident (e.g. payslips, tax records, accounts, order books).

2. Consider realistically (not pessimistically) what the future probably held if the accident had not happened:

   Assuming that your employer is still trading:

   (a) Would you still have the same job?

   (b) Would you have had a pay rise?

   (c) Might you have had a promotion. If so:-

       (i) Who was your competition?

       (ii) Why were you 'better'?

       (iii) Did you have periodic appraisals which would show how well you were doing?

       (iv) Who got the promotion?

   (d) Were you receiving employment benefits which are now lost: e.g. health insurance, use of vehicle, telephone?

   Assuming that your employer is not still trading:

   (e) What would you then have done if you had not been injured?

   (f) What were your chances of finding further work, and at what wage, and when, and where?

   (g) Might there have been increased or reduced travel costs in further work?

   (h) What qualifications did you have before the accident?

   (i) Can you still use any of those qualifications, or if not, is that because of the accident, or for some other reason?

   (j) What can you manage now?

   (k) Can you re-train in a field you know?

   (l) How long would re-training take, what would it cost, what is the rate of successful completion (something the college or provider should tell you), and what proportion of successful candidates find work?

   (m) Do you know what opportunities there may be?

(n) Could you re-train in a new field altogether?

(o) How long would re-training take, what would it cost, what is the rate of successful completion (something the college or provider should tell you), and what proportion of successful candidates find work?

(p) Do you know what opportunities there may be?

(q) What could you do if you did not pass the re-training course/exams?

VALUATION / PERSONAL CARE AND DOMESTIC ASSISTANCE

1. Keep a record (perhaps weekly) of the sort of personal care provided to you (noting particularly any unsocial hours). This may include help with: washing; dressing; toileting; changing dressings, etc.

2. Keep a record of tasks which others carry out for you. Typical examples are:
   (a) Cleaning;
   (b) Vacuuming;
   (c) Laundry and Ironing;
   (d) Cooking;
   (e) Gardening;
   (f) DIY/decorating;
   (g) Window cleaning;
   (h) Shopping;
   (i) Vehicle maintenance / cleaning.

3. Also, if you were excellent at an aspect of DIY or gardening etc., say so, and provide 'before photos' of work you had done, which demonstrate those capabilities. If you had not yet had the opportunity to use such skills, you will need to explain in more detail:
   (a) Whether you have any formal qualification (NVQ, etc.);
   (b) If not, then describe how you obtained the skill;
   (c) What you intended that skill to achieve.

4. Think as broadly as you can – you are simply trying to give a comprehensive picture of the likely impact of the accident upon you.

VALUATION / OTHER POTENTIAL CLAIMS

1. Do not miss important claims, but be sensible and realistic about whether the accident has actually caused the losses you are claiming.

2. Some further examples of relevant questions might be:
    (a) Will you need any extra equipment or furniture in your home?
    (b) Do you need an automatic vehicle?
    (c) Do you need an adapted vehicle?
    (d) Are you likely to incur additional travel costs?
    (e) Will conventional holidays be possible? If not, how can you be provided with holidays, and what additional costs might there be?

3. Again, think as broadly as you can – you are simply trying to give a comprehensive picture of the likely impact of the accident upon you.